One Stop Thematic Units

On the Move!

Transportation in God's World

Deborah Saathoff and Jane Jarrell

Illustrator
Dan Farris

Copyright © 1999 Jane C. Jarrell and Deborah L. Saathoff

Published by Concordia Publishing House
3558 S. Jefferson Avenue, St. Louis, MO 63118-3968
Manufactured in the United States of America

1   2   3   4   5   6   7   8   9   10   08 07 06 05 04 03 02 01 00 99

Contents

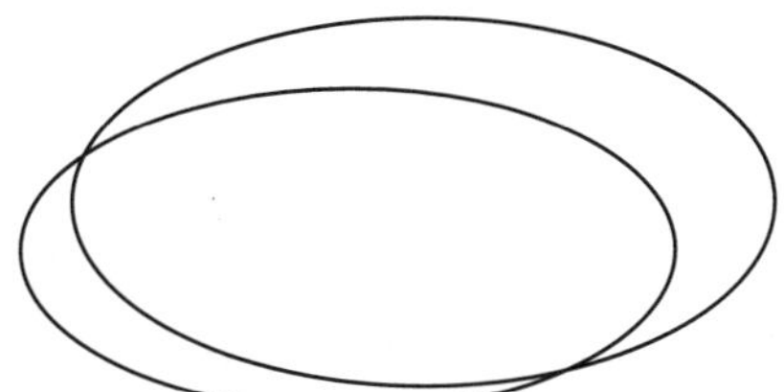

Dear Teachers and Parents,

On the Move is a collection of ideas for use in a transportation unit with young children. It is divided into four sections: In the Sky, In Trains, In Boats, and On the Highway. Each section contains suggestions and directions for your classroom in the following areas:

Room Decor: Creating a visual environment gives children the opportunity to instantly see what the theme is for a particular unit. It also helps to stimulate positive thoughts of making learning fun as soon as they walk into the room. An inspiring room decor opens their imagination to all the possibilities available to them as they begin to learn.

Story Time and Reading Center: *Blessed is he who keeps the words of the prophecy in this book* (Revelation 22:7). Opening a child's mind to reading, lays a foundation for learning that is unmatched. Opening a child's mind to the Bible, builds a foundation for eternity. A suggested list of books to match the theme is listed to share with the children and to leave available for their own exploration. (Please note that some of the books are out of print, but may still be available at libraries or in personal collections.)

Language and Alphabet Skills: A thematic approach to language and the alphabet gives children a great way to remember the basics. This section offers suggestions for activities, games, and ideas for stretching these basic skills.

Places to Go and People to See: This section helps make it all real by offering a "real life" approach to the lessons being shared. You will find many suggestions for field trips and guest speakers related to the theme.

Music! Music! Music!: *Speak to one another with psalms, hymns and spiritual songs. Sing and make music in your heart to the Lord* (Ephesians 5:19). Music makes a heart joyful. Music also enriches the learning opportunities for children. Learning thematic songs adds another dimension to each lesson.

Movement: Movement offers suggestions for active ways to experience the lesson being shared through exercise and games. It also gives everyone an opportunity to stretch, wiggle, and laugh. Movement encourages fun through thematic ideas for a break in the day.

Imaginative Play: Props and playthings that further enhance and encourage playing are suggested in this section. This offers the children an opportunity to really pretend to "be" and experience part of the theme.

Home Living Center: Here you will find suggestions for thematic additions to your year-round home living center.

Blocks Center: You will find suggestions for items to add and activities to encourage that build on the theme.

Sensory Table: The table you fill with sand, water, or other materials to encourage and build the exploration of the sense of touch can also be tailored to build on the theme. Included in this section are some suggestions for ways to do that.

Science: Some simple science experiments and explorations related to the theme are found in this section.

Math: Number recognition, one-to-one correspondence, counting, patterns, and shapes make up a preschooler's math curriculum. You will find thematic suggestions for these types of activities in this section.

Arts and Crafts: Instructions for items to make that relate to the theme.

Snack Time: This section offers recipes and suggestions for treats that build on the theme. Please note that the lists of ingredients only tell you the items needed, please adjust amounts according to your class size.

Faith Foundations: One way to make God's love appear real to a preschooler is through discussions about tangible things. The Faith Foundations apply Scripture to the lesson and include activities and questions to help further the discussion.

Ultimately, Faith Foundations becomes the center for all of the other ideas in hopes of helping to lead little ones to Christ. By no means is this considered the only place to build the faith of the little ones in your care. Simply pointing out to two friends working cooperatively in the blocks center, "I like the way you are working so nicely together. Isn't it wonderful that God gives us friends?" is just one way to integrate the reality of God and His love for us into every activity.

Use these ideas as printed, adapt them, pick and choose, or modify them to fit your needs. We hope this will be both a resource and a springboard of ideas that will be a blessing to you and your children.

Jane and Deborah

On the Move...
in the Sky

Airplanes, Helicopters, Hot Air Balloons, and Rockets

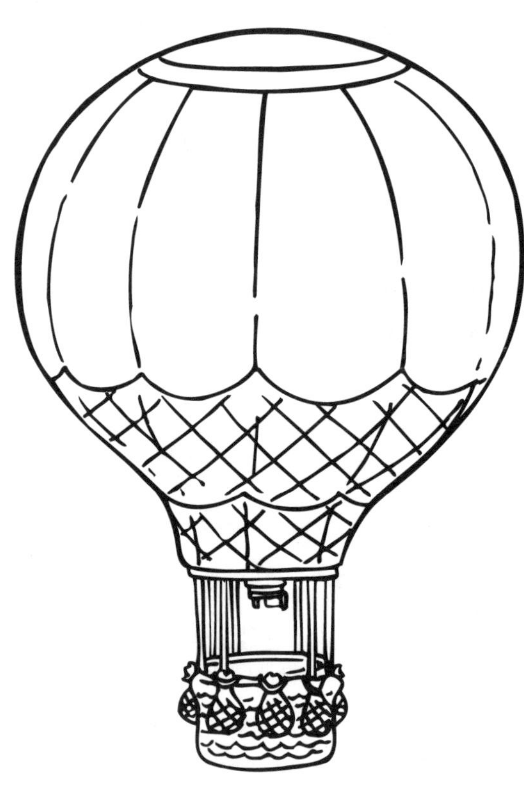

Room Decor

✔ Buy several inexpensive foam gliders, assemble them, and hang them from the ceiling. Intersperse cotton ball "clouds" among the planes.

✔ Display aerial photographs.

✔ Create a large cardboard propeller and put it on the door or a large wall space.

✔ Make hot air balloons one of your crafts (see arts and crafts section) and suspend the finished products from the ceiling.

✔ Make a giant hot air balloon for the door or a large wall space.

✔ Use the pattern provided (pages 8 and 9) to make your own border for a bulletin board.

Story Time and Reading Center

Barton, Byron. *Airplanes*

Barton, Byron. *Airport*

Bynnum, Janie. *Altoona Baboona*

Crews, Donald. *Flying*

Duchess of York. *Budgie at Bendick's Point*

Duchess of York. *Budgie the Little Helicopter*

Keats, Ezra Jack. *The Trip*

McPhail, David M. *First Flight*

*Mantegazza, Giovanna. *Look inside an Airplane*

*Petty, Kate. *On a Plane*

*Potter, Tony. *See How It Works: Planes*

Rey, Margret and H. A. and Vipah Interactive. *Margret and H. A. Rey's Curious George and the Hot Air Balloon*

Robb, Andy. *Polly Plane* (CPH 1999)

Rockwell, Anne F. *Planes*

*Rogers, Fred. *Going on an Airplane*

Siebert, Diane. *Plane Song*

This book is out of print but may still be available through the Internet, in libraries, or in personal collections.

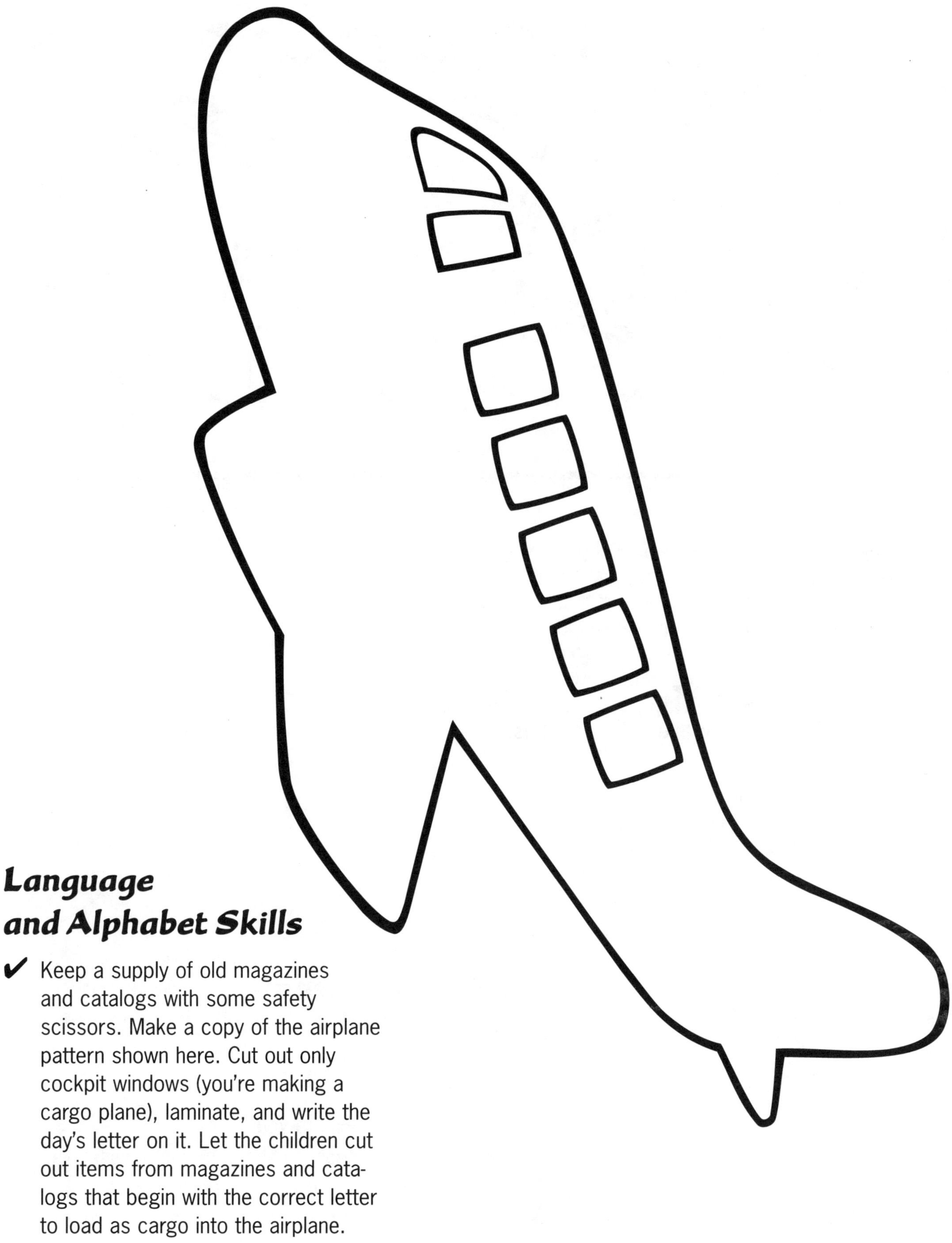

Language
and Alphabet Skills

✔ Keep a supply of old magazines
and catalogs with some safety
scissors. Make a copy of the airplane
pattern shown here. Cut out only
cockpit windows (you're making a
cargo plane), laminate, and write the
day's letter on it. Let the children cut
out items from magazines and catalogs that begin with the correct letter
to load as cargo into the airplane.

✔ Play the alphabet game with an airplane variation.
The first person begins by saying, "I'm going to fly
on an airplane and I'm going to take an anteater
(or some other noun beginning with the letter "a").
The next person would follow with, "I'm going on
an airplane and I'm going to take a balloon (or other
noun beginning with "b"). This continues around the
circle until all letters of the alphabet are used.

Places to Go and People to See

✘ Visit an airport.

✘ Visit a flight museum.

✘ Tour a hangar.

✘ Invite a pilot to speak to your class.

✘ Invite a flight attendant to speak to your class.

✘ Invite an airline mechanic to speak to your class.

✘ Invite a member of the Air Force to speak to your class.

Up, Up and Away
(In My Beautiful Balloon)

Since there aren't many airplane songs for young children, improvise the lyrics to some old favorites.

Fly, Fly, Fly the Plane

Melody: *"Row, Row, Row Your Boat"*
Fly, fly, fly the plane,
Fly the plane so high.
Merrily, merrily, merrily, merrily,
Soaring through the sky.

I'm a Little Airplane

Melody: *"I'm A Little Teapot"*
I'm a little airplane,
See me fly.
Up where the clouds are
High in the sky.
I am soaring over
Towns below.
Lift your eyes to watch me go!

She'll Be Flying an Airplane/
He'll Be Flying a Chopper

Melody: *"She'll Be Comin' Round the Mountain"*
She'll be flying an airplane when she comes.
She'll be flying an airplane when she comes.
She'll be flying an airplane,
She'll be flying an airplane,
She'll be flying an airplane when she comes.
He'll be flying a chopper when he comes.
He'll be flying a chopper when he comes.
He'll be flying a chopper,
He'll be flying a chopper,
He'll be flying a chopper when he comes.

Movement

✔ Pretend to be airplanes sitting on the runway. Taxi down the runway. Fly into the sky. Soar through the air. Land. Taxi to a stop. Pull into the hangar.

✔ Pretend to be hot air balloons rolled up and stored away. Unroll. Slowly lift as you fill with air. "Float" gently through the air. Land. Deflate. Roll back up.

✔ Pretend to be rockets ready for take off. Count down from 10 to blastoff. Slowly lift the rocket through the atmosphere. Orbit the earth. Slowly reenter the atmosphere. Splash down! (Or land, if you would like to be space shuttles.)

Imaginative Play

✗ Pilot hats
✗ Pilot wings (often available from airlines)
✗ Small suitcases on wheels
✗ Goggles
✗ Scarves
✗ Tickets and boarding passes
✗ Travel brochures
✗ Matchbox or other small airplanes and helicopters
✗ Fisher Price Little People airplane set

✗ Dashboard (see arts and crafts for instructions)

✗ Set up an airplane by creating a designated "cockpit" and then setting up chairs in rows similar to those on an airplane.

✗ Make airplanes from cardboard boxes large enough to fit around a child. Tape the boxes closed. Cut a space from the center large enough for a child to stand in. Attach cardboard wings to the sides of the box. Attach rope or straps to the box to fit over the child's shoulders and hang about waist high.

Space Imaginative Play

- ✗ Old computer
- ✗ Space pictures
- ✗ Backpacks as space packs
- ✗ Old 2-liter soda bottles as oxygen tanks
- ✗ Helmets made from upside-down brown grocery bags, clear plastic milk jugs with handles removed, or upside-down ice cream containers with a rectangle cut out
- ✗ A large, sturdy (appliance size) cardboard box as a child-size rocket (Cut the top flaps into triangles and bring together in a point. Secure with package tape. Cut out a door. Make triangular fins using extra cardboard from top flaps. Cover the rocket with aluminum foil.)
- ✗ Two sheets sewn together and stuffed with foam blocks as the bouncy moon surface

Blocks Center

- ✗ Add toy airplanes and helicopters to the block area. Build runways, hangars, and helicopter landing pads with the blocks.
- ✗ Add small astronauts, rockets, satellites, etc. Build rockets for the astronauts or launch pads for the rockets.

Home Living Center

- ✗ Suitcases
- ✗ Tickets
- ✗ Travel brochures

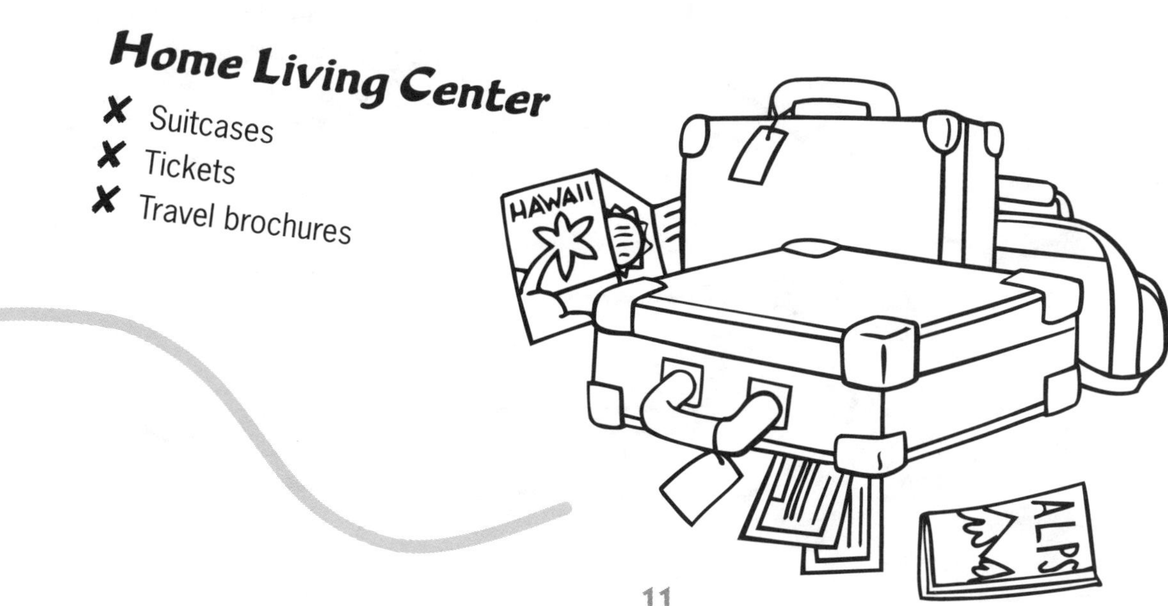

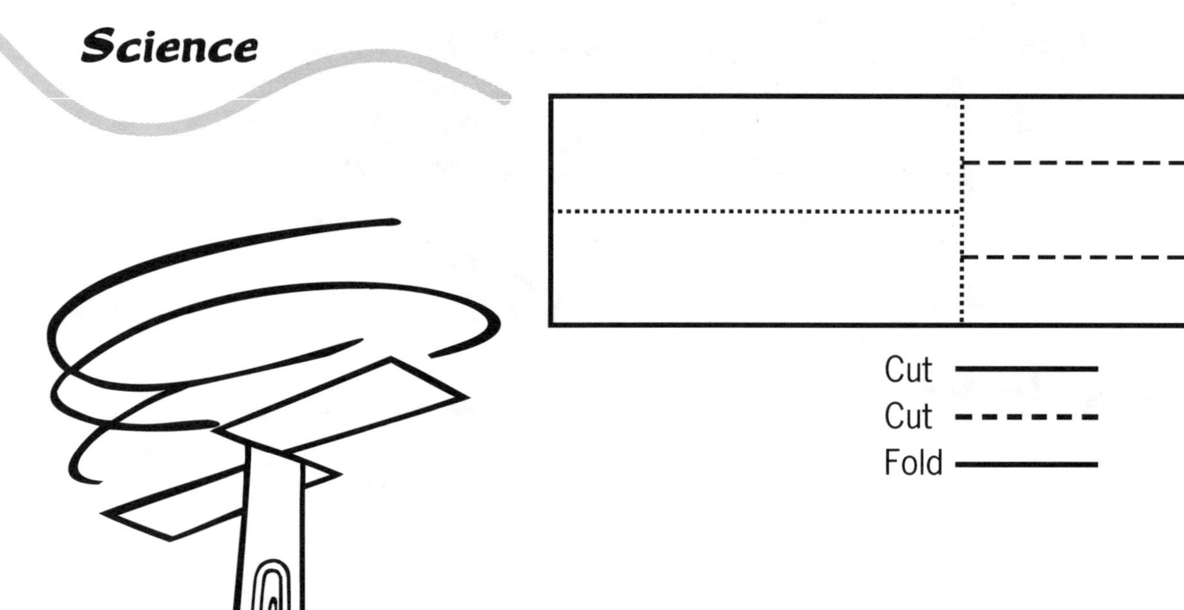

Cut ——————

Cut - - - - - -

Fold ——————

Spinner Helicopters

These operate along the same lines as the rotary blade of a helicopter and are based on ash or maple seeds. Copy and cut as shown in the diagram above. Hold the spinners as high as you can, drop them, and watch them fall. Note what happens. Collect maple or ash seeds and compare. Experiment by adding more paper clips or removing paper clips.

Styrofoam Gliders

You Will Need:

Styrofoam meat or vegetable trays

X-Acto knife

Pencil

Paper clips

How to Do:

1. Trace the patterns for gliders (shown below) onto Styrofoam trays.
2. Cut the shapes using an X-Acto knife.
3. Carefully cut out the slot for the wings.
4. Place the wing through the slot and center.
5. Place a paper clip on the nose to add stability. Experiment to find the best location for the paper clip.
6. Release the gliders from a high spot and watch them float down.

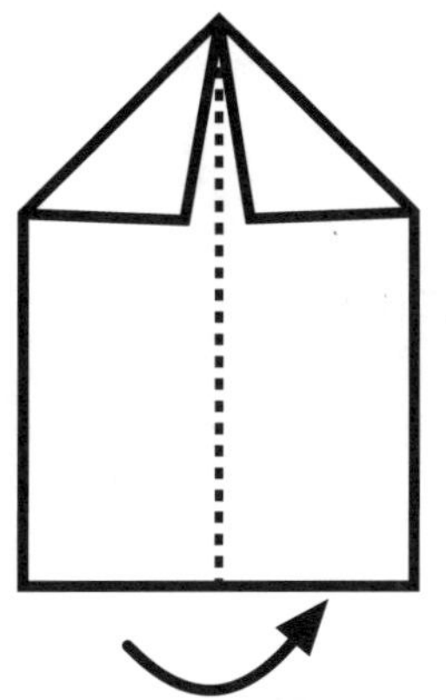

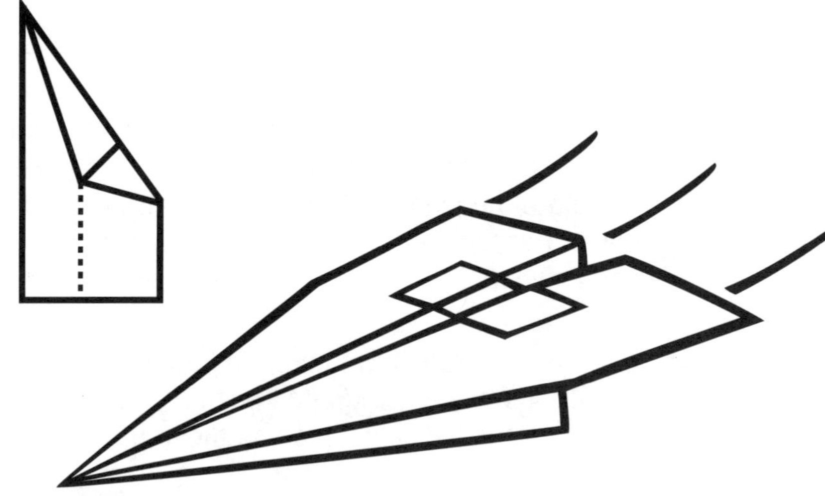

Airplanes

Make paper airplanes using the diagram or substitute your favorite method. Experiment with different nose weights, wings, etc. Fly the airplanes.

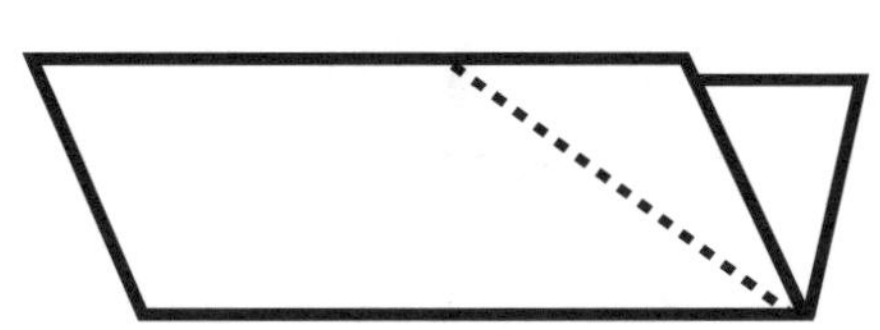
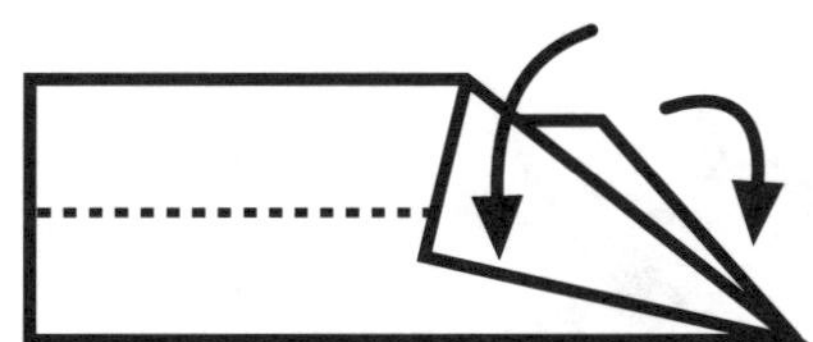
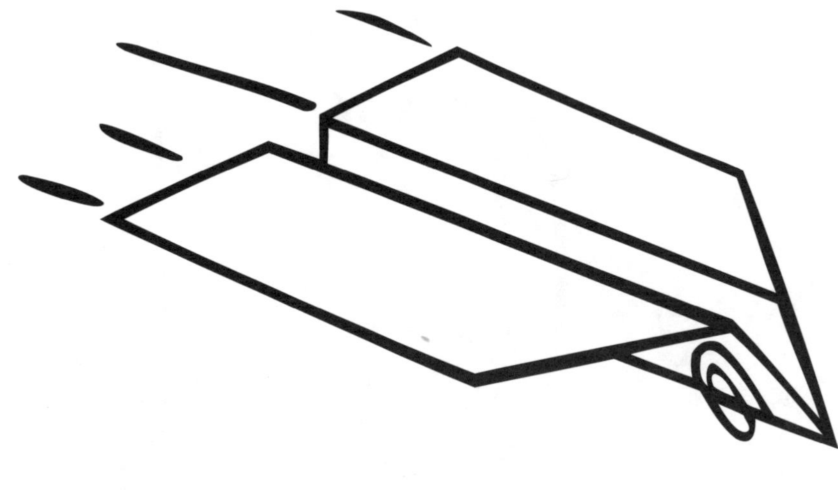

Inflating Balloons with (Sort of) Hot Air

You Will Need:

16 oz. clear soda bottle

¼ cup vinegar

¼ cup baking soda

Uninflated balloon

Funnel

How to Do:

1. Pour the vinegar into the soda bottle.
2. Using the funnel, spoon the baking soda into the balloon.
3. Make sure no baking soda is left around the mouth of the balloon.
4. Carefully attach the mouth of the balloon to the neck of the soda bottle.
5. Turn the balloon up and shake the baking soda into the bottle.
6. Watch the reaction of the baking soda and vinegar produce gas that inflates the balloon.

Math

✔ Use the pattern (page 7) to make several airplanes. Cut out cockpit and passenger windows. Write a numeral on each airplane equal to or less than the number of windows. Laminate the planes. Have the children guess the correct number of passengers in the plane. Passengers could be counters, pictures of people's faces cut out of magazines and laminated, or even photographs of the children in the class cut out and laminated.

✔ Use the pattern (shown here) and construction paper to make several colorful hot air balloons. Write a numeral on each basket. Have the children put the correct number of dots (round stickers such as those used for garage sale pricing) on each balloon.

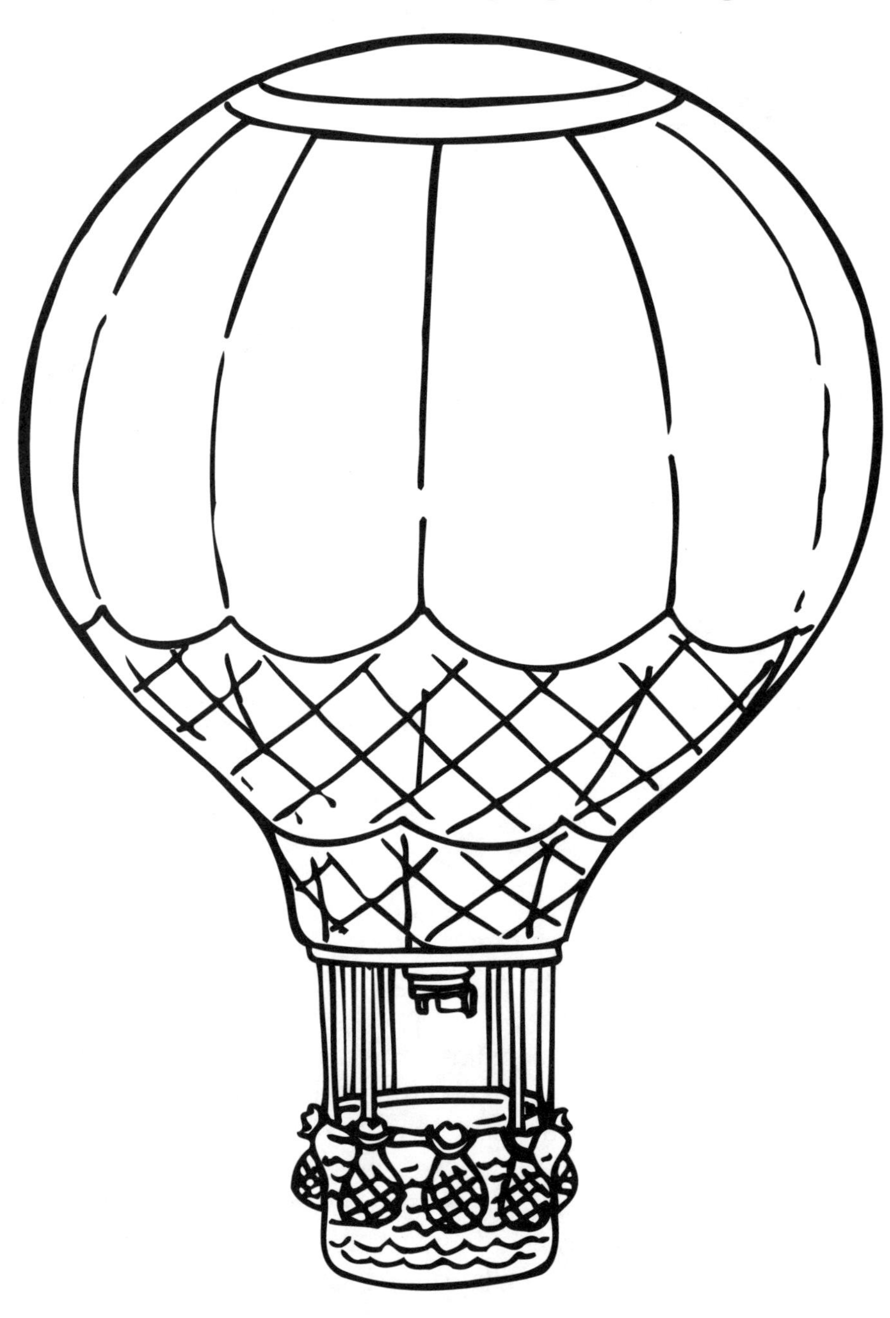

✔ Make an equal number of balloons and baskets. Decorate the balloon with a number of circles or round stickers. On a corresponding basket, write the number of dots. Let the children match the numeral on the basket with the correct number of dots on the balloon.

✔ Do a simple graphing activity using a single piece of chart paper at the front of the room. Make several shapes (airplane, helicopter, or hot air balloon as long as all are the same) of three or four different colors. Ask the children to pick the one that is the color they like the best. Then have the children place their shape in its appropriate column of the graph paper. Ask them about the results. (For example: "Which color was chosen by four children? How many children chose red?") Vary the activity by making an airplane, a helicopter, and a hot air balloon all the same color. (Ask: "Which mode of transportation was chosen by the most children?")

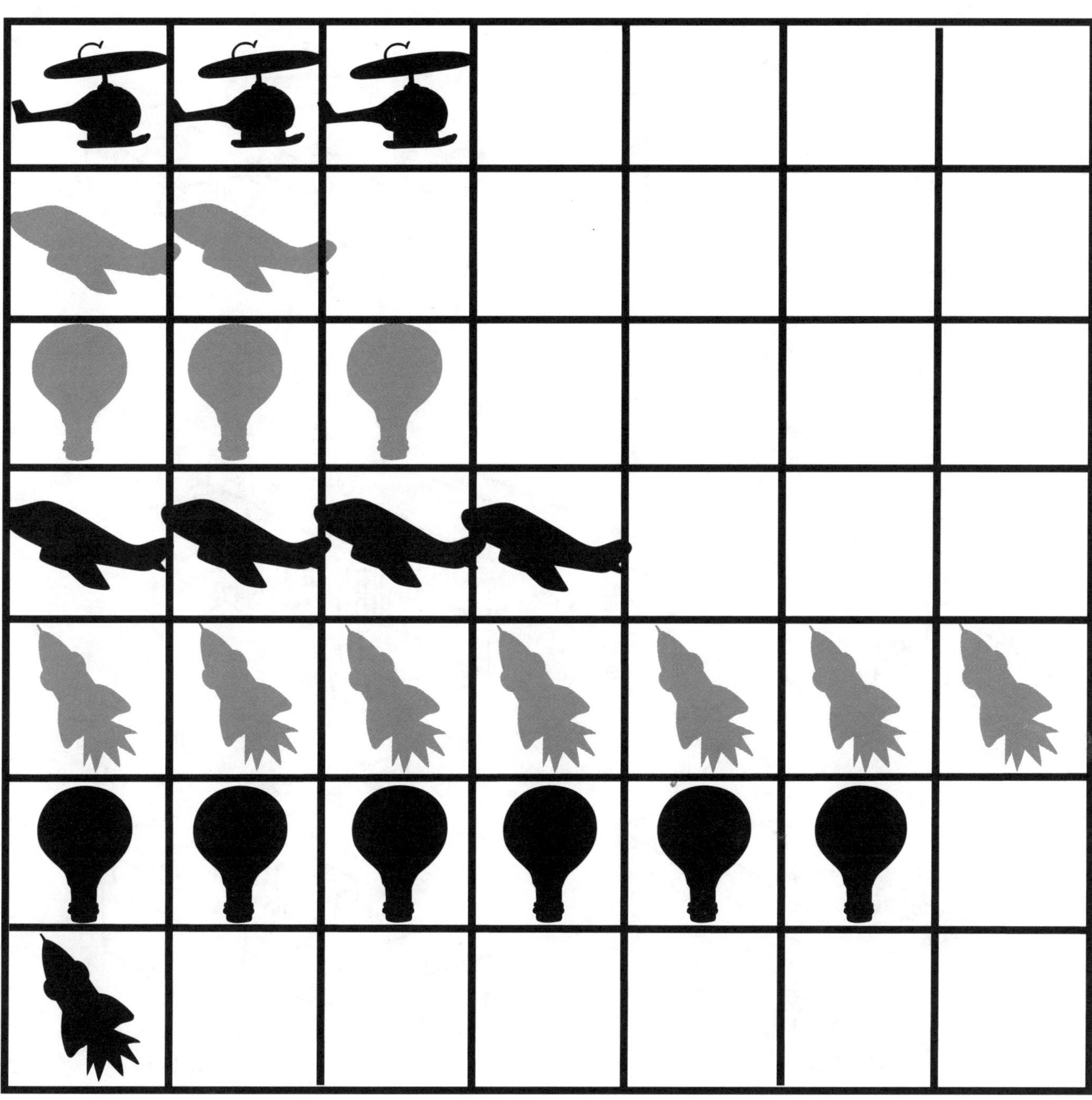

Arts and Crafts

Shoebox City (to accompany the story *The Trip* by Ezra Jack Keats)

You Will Need:

Shoebox
Scissors
Construction paper
Tape
Plastic wrap

How to Do:

1. Cut out a hole in the front of the shoebox.
2. Cut out the back of the box and make a window in the top of the box.
3. Cut out shapes of tall buildings and tape to the bottom of the shoebox.
4. Tape the plastic wrap over the window on the top.
5. Tape the back part of the box with construction paper.
6. Look at your city through the hole cut in the front of the box.

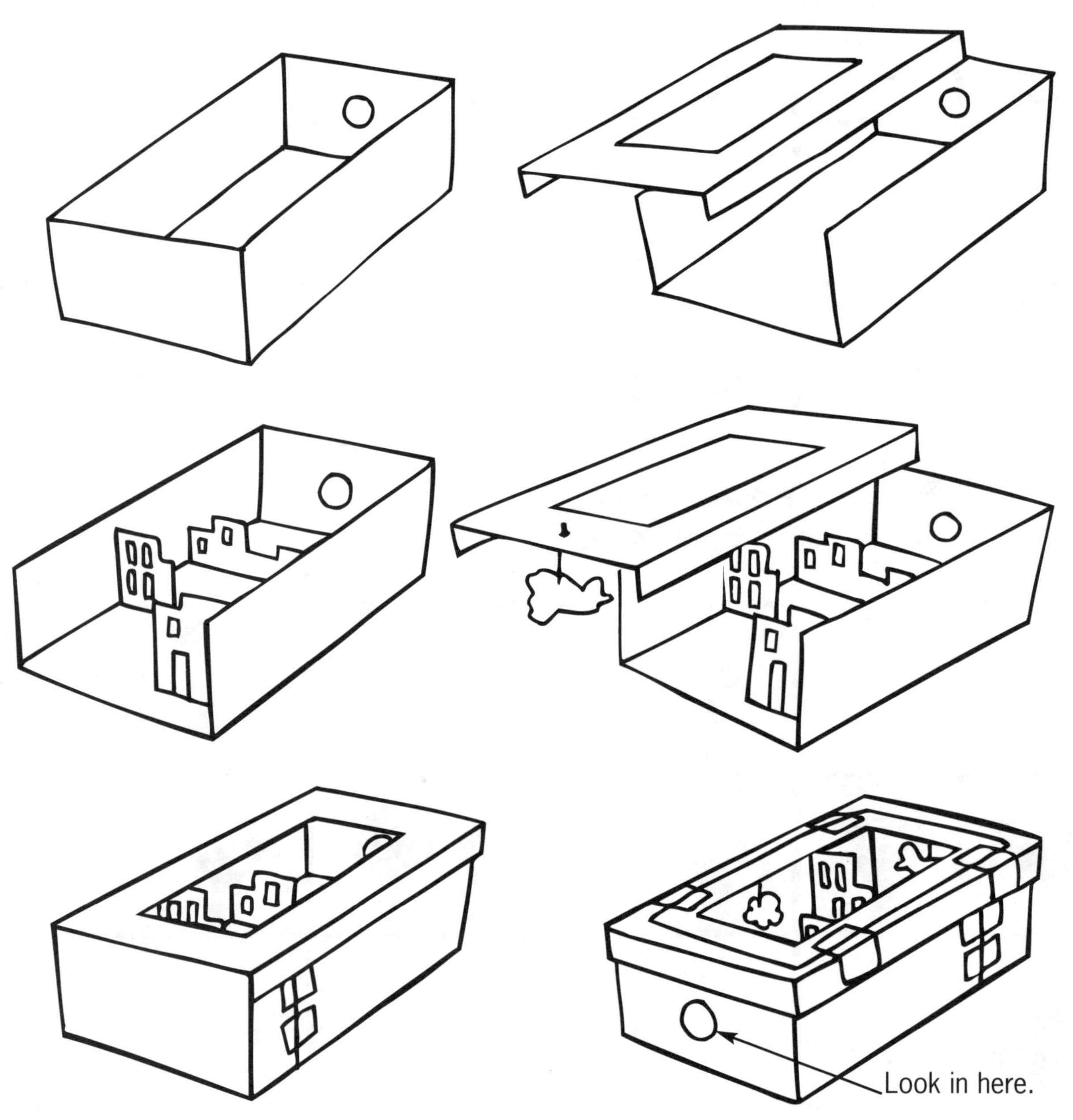

Dashboard

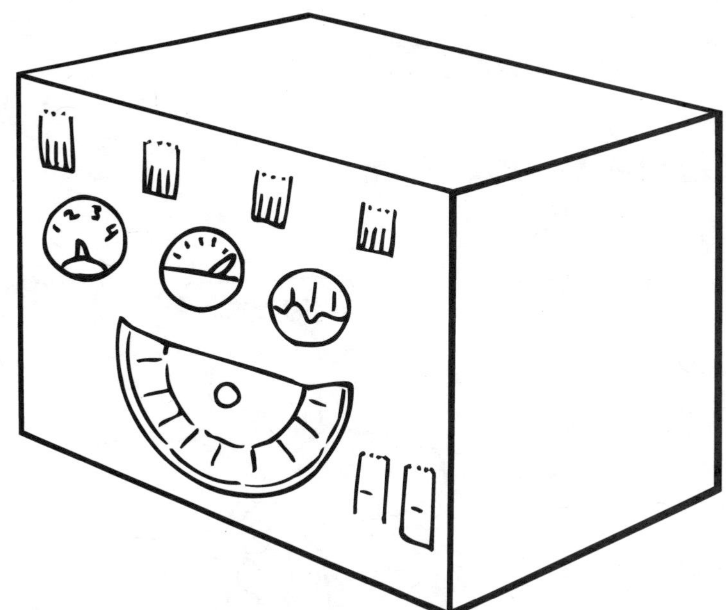

You Will Need:

Sturdy cardboard box, at least 18″ wide

Brass fasteners

Scissors

Glue

Crayons or markers

Aluminum pie plate or large paper plate
  (cut in half for a more aeronautical look)

Assorted colors of construction paper
  or various plastic container lids

How to Do:

1. Turn the box upside down so you will have a flat surface to work on.
2. Poke a hole in the center of the aluminum pie plate and secure it to the box with a brass fastener.
3. Cut out several construction paper circles and write numerals around the perimeter.
   Draw a dial in the center for the speedometer and other dials.
4. Glue those above and to either side of the wheel.
5. Cut out three sides of small rectangles from the box in various places to create switches.
6. Once the dashboard is dry, turn it on its side.
7. Prepare for take off!

Hot Air Balloons

You Will Need:

Balloons

Newspaper strips

Glue

Pint-size fruit baskets

Yarn (enough for two 48″ pieces per student)

Washable paint

Paintbrushes

Scissors

How to Do:

1. Make papier-maché balloons by wrapping strips of newspaper,
   soaked in thin glue, around the balloons. Cover the balloons
   completely. Allow them to dry.
2. Paint the balloons.
3. Tie the pieces of yarn together in the middle. Glue to the top
   of the balloon.
4. Bring the ends of the yarn down around the balloon.
   Tie to the four corners of the fruit basket.
5. Add a small toy or stuffed animal.
6. Hang your balloons from the ceiling.

* You can vary this activity by replacing the newspaper and paint with strips of tissue paper.

Cracker Snacker Plane

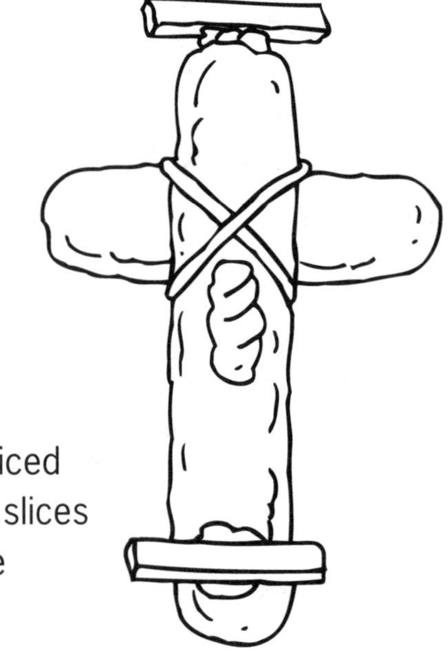

You Will Need:
Wax paper
Knife
Cutting board
Carrot peeler

Ingredients:
Breadsticks
String cheese
Carrot, peeled, sliced
 and cut into ¼″ slices
Squirtable cheese

How to Do:
1. Place the bread stick on a piece of wax paper.
2. Take a second breadstick and break it in half. Place it about 1″ down from the top of the first breadstick.
3. Pull the string cheese apart. Tie the two bread sticks together by wrapping the string cheese around the two sticks, forming the shape of an airplane.
4. Cut the carrot slices in half.
5. Squirt a little cheese on the front tip of the breadstick. Place the half carrot on the cheese to form a propeller.
6. Squirt a little cheese on the top back part of the longer breadstick.
7. Place a half carrot slice on the cheese to form the back rudder of the airplane.

* Carrots can be affixed for the wing propellers and tires too.

Hot Air Balloon Treats

Use a round cookie for the balloon, string licorice for the ropes, and half of a wafer cookie for the basket.

Enjoy!

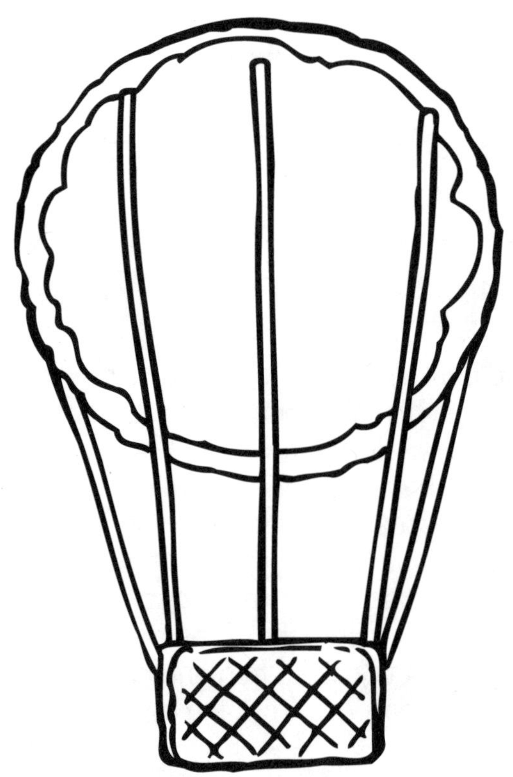

Faith Foundations

As we fly through the skies or as we look up from our places on the ground at the skies above, we are reminded of the greatness, the majesty of our God. To build faith foundations in our children as we talk about moving through the skies, include time to reflect on what those skies declare to us.

Scripture Foundation

The heavens declare the glory of God; the skies proclaim the work of His hands. Day after day they pour forth speech; night after night they display knowledge. There is no speech or language where their voice is not heard. Their voice goes out into all the earth, their words to the ends of the world (Psalm 19:1–4).

Questions

Q What do we see in the sky that shows us how wonderful God is?

Q What do we see in the sky that shows us how great and big God is?

Q If the things we see in the sky don't have words, how do they speak to us about God?

God made two great lights—the greater light to govern the day and the lesser light to govern the night. He also made the stars. God set them in the expanse of the sky to give light on the earth, to govern the day and the night, and to separate light from darkness. And God saw that it was good (Genesis 1:16–18).

The sun and the moon are two ever-present testimonies to our Amazing Creator.

Sun Activities

✘ On a sunny day, find a window that has a shade or blind. Hold your hand up to the window behind the shade or blind. Now lift the shade or blind and hold your hand up to the window again. Your hand feels warmer, not because you touched anything, but because you felt the heat of the sun—a star 93 million miles away from us. God put the sun in the sky to warm us. List all of the blessings we receive because the sun shines.

✘ Use the sun to make an art project. Take light-sensitive paper found at nature center gift shops or toy and hobby shops and arrange leaves, flowers, or other objects on the piece of paper. (Some light-sensitive paper comes in kits with a piece of plexiglass to place on top to hold the objects in place.) Expose the paper and objects to light for about five minutes, remove the objects, and put the paper in water to set the image. The paper will be white where the objects were placed and the rest of the background will be a dark blue.

Moon Activity

✘ While the sun looks much the same in the sky wherever it may be, the moon changes a little bit each night. Ask your children to check on the changes of the moon every night. The reason for the phases of the moon is that the moon does not create its own light, it reflects the light of the sun. Sometimes our earth gets in the way and blocks part of the sun, creating a shadow on the moon. You can make a flip book by making a copy of the pattern (page 20) showing the phases of the moon, cutting the pictures apart, and pasting them onto plain white index cards or pieces of tagboard. Put the cards in order with the first picture on top. Staple the left-hand side of the cards together, then flip through the pages to watch how the moon changes.

Star Activity

✘ Sponge paint white stars on black construction paper. Arrange them in constellations if you wish. Add a little glitter to the paint before you sponge to create sparkling stars.

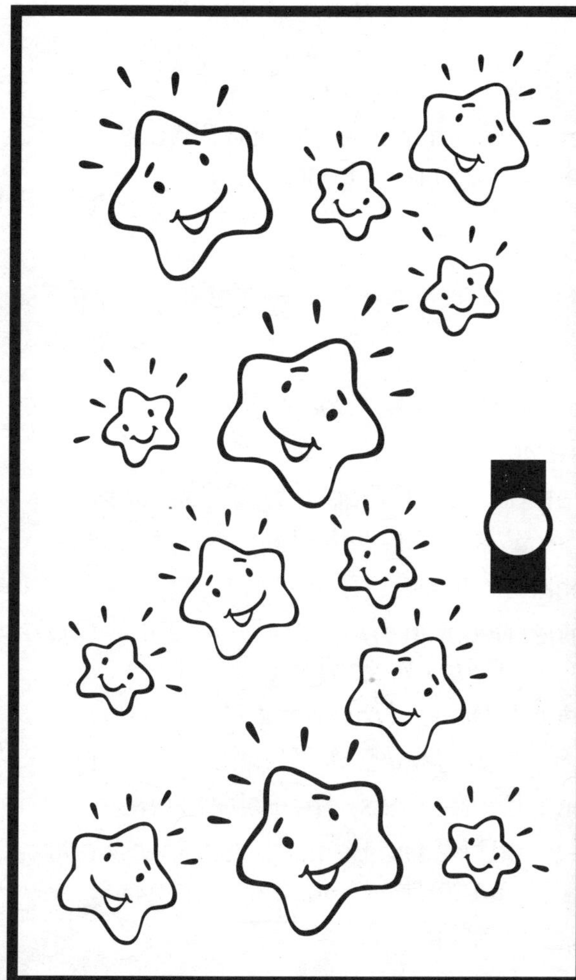

Rainbow Activities

God set His rainbow in the sky as a reminder of His promise to Noah never to flood the whole earth again. The rainbow in the sky helps us remember that God always keeps His promises. As you do the activities, talk about the promises of God we should remember. (*I am with you always. For God so loved the world. I will never leave you nor forsake you. I will send [the Holy Spirit] to you.*)

✘ Create a rainbow with a garden hose. On a sunny day (early morning or late afternoon are the best times because the sun's rays are the most slanted), stand with your back to the sun and spray a fine mist in front of you. Try to find a dark background for the spray so the colors really stand out.

✘ Make an indoor rainbow using a prism. Hang a prism from the window. Prisms also work in darkened rooms. Pull the shades to allow for only a small beam of the light to shine (windows facing south are best). Put your prism in the path of light and project a rainbow onto the opposite wall.

✘ Make your own prism. Fill a glass all the way to the top with water. Set it on a windowsill in bright sunlight. The bottom of the glass should extend somewhat over the window ledge. Put a piece of white paper on the floor beneath the window and a rainbow should appear.

Just think, God makes the rainbows across the skies using the sun He created and the rain He sends!

On the Move ... in Trains

Room Decor

✔ Lay masking tape railroad tracks along pathways.

✔ Put a large front view of a locomotive on the door.

✔ Decorate around walls by putting a lo-o-o-ong train running around the room. Put photographs of the children in the train cars.

✔ Bring a real railroad tie to the room.

✔ Use the pattern provided (pages 24 and 25) and make your own border for a bulletin board.

Story Time and Reading Center

Barton, Byron. *Trains*

*Brown, Margaret Wise. *Two Little Trains*

Brown, Margaret Wise. *The Train to Timbuctoo*

Burton, Virginia Lee. *Choo Choo*

Crampton, Gertrude. *Tootle*

Crews, Donald. *Freight Train*

Crews, Donald. *Shortcut*

Gibbons, Gail. *Trains*

*Greene, Graham. *The Little Train*

*Gretz, Susanna and Alison Sage. *Teddy Bears Take the Train*

McPhail, David M. *The Train*

*Maestro, Betsy and Guilio. *All Aboard Overnight*

Magee, Doug. *All Aboard ABC*

*Martin, Bill. *Smoky Poky*

Peet, Bill. *The Caboose Who Got Loose*

Piper, Watty. *The Little Engine that Could*

Rockwell, Anne F. *Trains*

Shine, Deborah. *The Little Engine that Could Pudgy Word Book*

Siebert, Diane. *Train Song*

Stevenson, James. *All Aboard!*

Van Allsburg, Chris. *The Polar Express*

Westcott, Nadine Bernard. *I've Been Working on the Railroad*

*This book is out of print, but may still be available through the Internet, in libraries, or in personal collections.

Make an Alphabet Train

You Will Need:

Scissors

27 empty ½ pint milk cartons

Self-adhesive Contact paper or
   construction paper or gift wrap

Empty box from kitchen matches

Glue

Markers

Yarn

Stapler

Empty Spool

How to Do:

1. Cut off the top of each milk carton.
2. Cover the sides of the milk carton with the self-adhesive paper.
   If using construction paper or giftwrap, glue it in place.
3. These are your alphabet train cars.
4. Cut out small circles of black construction paper for the wheels and glue two on each car.
5. Cut out 26 white circles and write, stamp, or sticker each white circle with a different letter
   of the alphabet.
6. Cut 26 pieces of yarn about 4″ in length. Staple to each end of the boxcars, connecting all
   of the cars in alphabetical order.
7. Make the train engine by covering the matchbox with paper. Turn the carton upside down
   and glue a spool on top for the smokestack. Attach the wheels.
8. Find small objects around the room and place them into the car labeled with the first letter
   of the item.
9. You can also cut out pictures from magazines and place them into the alphabet boxcar
   that matches the first letter in its name.
10. Modify the alphabet train by making the train cars out of file folders, either stapled along
    the sides or laminated with the top opening cut. Label each car with a letter of the
    alphabet. Let the children cut out magazine or catalog pictures to place into the
    train car that matches the letter of the alphabet.

✔ Change the alphabet train activity into a matching activity
   by providing laminated pictures to slide into the train cars.

✔ Play the alphabet game with a train theme. Let the first person say, "I'm going on a train ride and
   I'm going to take an alligator" (or some other noun beginning with "a"). The next person would say,
   "I'm going to take a train ride and I'm going to take a bathtub" (or any noun beginning with "b").
   Continue through the alphabet.

Places to Go and People to See

✗ Visit a train station.

✗ Take a train ride.

✗ Visit a railroad museum.

✗ Visit a hobby shop to see a miniature railroad.

✗ Visit a factory or plant that uses trains for supply and watch them load or unload the trains.

✗ Invite an engineer or railroad worker to speak to your class.

✗ Invite someone who collects model trains to share the collection with your class.

Music! Music! Music!

"I've Been Working on the Railroad"
"Little Red Caboose"
"Down by the Station"
"Chattanooga Choo Choo"
"Rock Island Line"
"This Train Is Bound for Glory"

Modify some old familiar tunes with a train theme.

Here We Go Riding on the Train

Melody: *"Here We Go Round the Mulberry Bush"*

Here we go riding on the train,
On the train, on the train.
Here we go riding on the train,
So early in the morning.

Movement

✔ Form a classroom train by having the children form a line with each child holding the shoulders or waist of the person directly in front. Chug around the classroom, school, or play yard. The "locomotive" could blow a train whistle (found in hobby shops) or you could listen to train songs as you go.

✔ Let each child pretend to be "Tootle" or the "Little Engine that Could." Or just let them pretend to be locomotives.

✔ Pull slowly away from the engine house. Chug slowly uphill, working hard. Roll quickly downhill puffing happily. Stop to collect a load. Pull away, slowly pulling your load. Chug over to a new location to deliver your load. Chug back home to the engine house.

Imaginative Play

X Engineer caps

X Gloves

X Bandanas

X Train whistles (available at hobby and some toy stores)

X Toy trains

X Tickets

X Train schedules

X Hole punch (for conductors)

X Laundry basket train (baskets tied together with rope) to use with toys or stuffed animals

Home Living Center

X Briefcase and newspaper (to carry on the train)

X Suitcases

X Tickets and train schedules

X Maps of train routes

X Trays and play food to help create a train dining car

Blocks Center

X Add toy trains to roll along block tracks.

X Make station houses, tunnels, and bridges.

X Add large train cars to be loaded with blocks.

Science

✔ Use two identical toy trains to explore the question "Does the longer (heavier) train roll farther?"

How to Do:

1. Set up a long inclined plane, one that will allow you to place a single locomotive evenly with one carrying three or four train cars.

2. Mark a start line with tape.

3. Let the two trains go at the same time.

✔ Ask the children questions such as "Which one rolls farther?" "Does it roll farther every time? Why?" "What rule can we make up for our trains?"

✔ Line up the trains evenly on a flat surface and give them a push. Is the same rule true? Why or why not?

✔ Vary the activity by comparing the distance the trains roll down the inclined ramp onto carpet and then onto a tile floor. Or vary the height of the ramp and compare distances.

Math

✔ Draw faces on several Popsicle sticks to make people. Put a train of small boxes together with a numeral on each box. Put the correct number of people into each train car.

✔ Use the pattern (on these facing pages) to make a 1 to 10 train. Put the numeral 1 on the locomotive, then number the remaining cars 2 through 10. For younger children use dots or pictures and use numerals or words for older children. Let the children put the cars in order.

✔ Use the pattern to make pattern trains. Offer laminated train cars in three or four colors. Have the children either match patterns you make or create their own patterns.

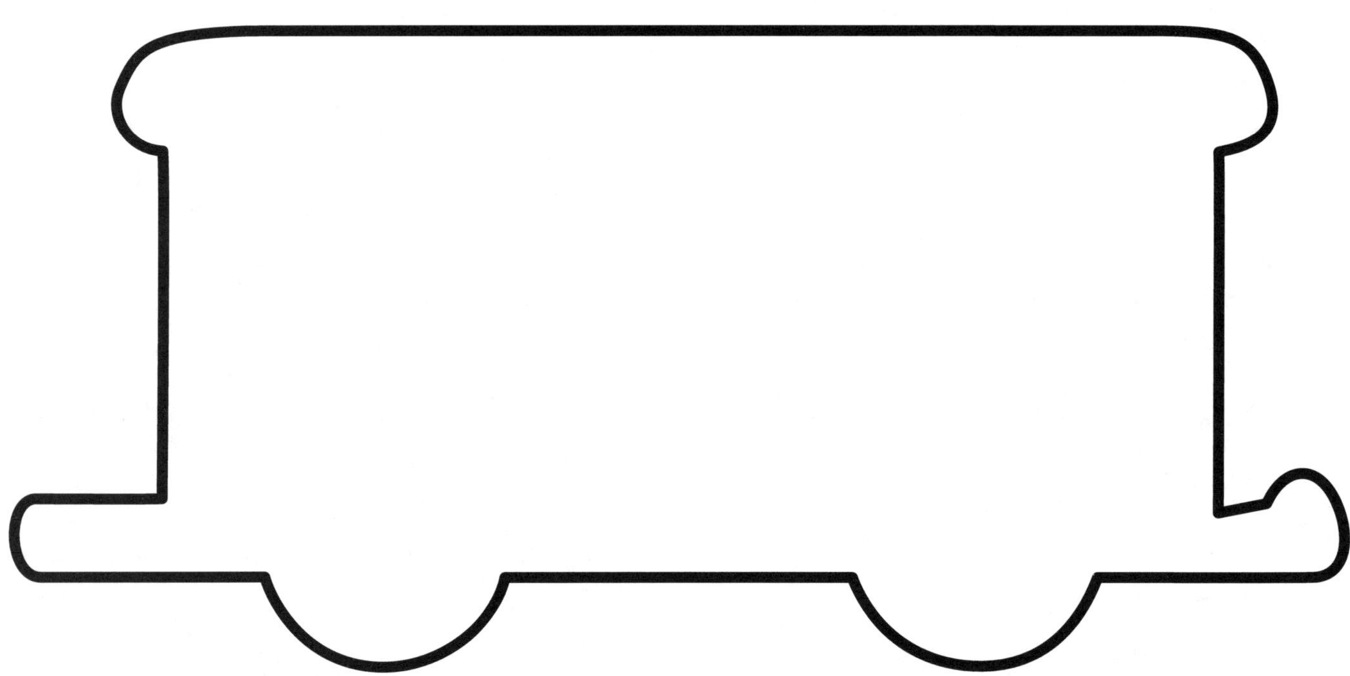

Egg Carton Train

You Will Need:

1 egg carton for every two children

1 cardboard toilet tissue tube
  for every two children

Washable paint

Paintbrushes

Scissors

How to Do:

1. Cut an egg carton into two strips of six egg cups each.
2. Cut the toilet tissue tube in half.
3. Place one half of the toilet tissue tube on the first egg cup in the line.
4. Glue in place to make the locomotive.
5. Paint the train.

Railroad Track Prints

You Will Need:

Sections of railroad tracks from toy
  or model train sets

Washable paint

Paper

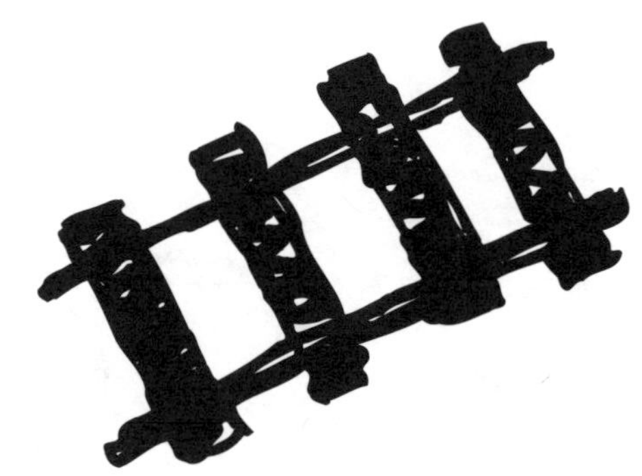

How to Do:

1. Mix the paint to a rather thick consistency.
2. Let the children place a section of track in the paint
   and then print the design onto paper.
3. After the paint has dried completely, the children could
   run their play dough train creations on the tracks.
   See the recipe on the next page for a play dough train variation.

Colorful Cookie Train

You Will Need:

Wax paper
Rolling pin
Train-shaped cookie cutters
Cookie sheet
Knife

Ingredients:

Prepared sugar cookie dough
Red licorice twists
Red, orange, yellow, green, blue, purple, black icings

How to Do:

1. Place wax paper on the counter top.
2. Lightly sprinkle with flour.
3. Place the sugar cookie dough on the floured surface and roll to a ⅜" thickness.
4. Using the cookie cutters, cut the dough into train shapes. Place on cookie sheet and bake according to package directions. Cool.
5. Place the baked train shapes onto wax paper and decorate each train car with the colored icings.
6. Cut the red licorice into 1" long pieces and place between the sugar cookie cars.

* Try this project with different colors of play dough for an art activity.

Cracker Snacker Train

You Will Need:

Wax paper
Cookie sheet
Vegetable scraper
Cutting board
Knife

Ingredients:

Saltine crackers
Creamy peanut butter
Carrots, washed, peeled, and cut into ¼" slices
Little wheat crackers
Carrot sticks
Celery sticks
Candy-coated chocolates

How to Do:

1. Make cracker boxes out of five saltine crackers (four for the sides and one for the bottom). Use peanut butter to glue the edges of the sides together. Repeat this four times. Three of the cracker boxes will be the boxcars and the fourth will become the engine.
2. Place the cracker boxcars in a line on the cookie sheet. Place a carrot stick between each boxcar to join the cars together.
3. For the fourth boxcar, place a little peanut butter around the top edges of the cracker and stick a sixth cracker on the top, giving the "engine" a lid.
4. Form another six-cracker box with the small wheat crackers. Place this on top of the "engine" cracker box to form the cab of the freight train.
5. Place the carrot slices on the sides of the cracker boxes to form the wheels.
6. Behind the cab of the train, glue half of a bread stick with peanut butter to form the smokestack.
7. Fill the boxcars with carrot sticks, celery sticks, and candy-coated chocolates.

* Try making a railroad track out of red licorice. Make two straight lines with the licorice. Using kitchen scissors, cut smaller pieces of licorice to place between the long pieces, forming the railroad ties.

Subway Train

You Will Need:
Cutting board
Knife

Ingredients:
Soft French bread loaves
String cheese

How to Do:
1. Cut each loaf of bread into four wide slices and place on a cookie sheet.
2. Separate the string cheese into long strings.
3. Turn each bread slice on its side and cut a square out of the side, forming subway windows. If you cut the square all the way through to the other side, it will make a great place for sandwich fixings.
4. Place the bread slices several inches apart on the cookie sheet. Place the strings of cheese between each piece of bread to connect the bread "cars."

Pretzel Stick Train Track

You Will Need:
Wax paper

Ingredients:
Stick pretzels
Peanut butter

How to Do:
1. Place the pretzel sticks in two straight lines, making the lines far enough apart to place "railroad ties" crosswise down the center.
2. Use peanut butter, if needed, to stick the railroad ties to the tracks.

Cheese Railroad Tracks

You Will Need:
Squirtable cheese
Wax paper
Cookie sheet
Crackers

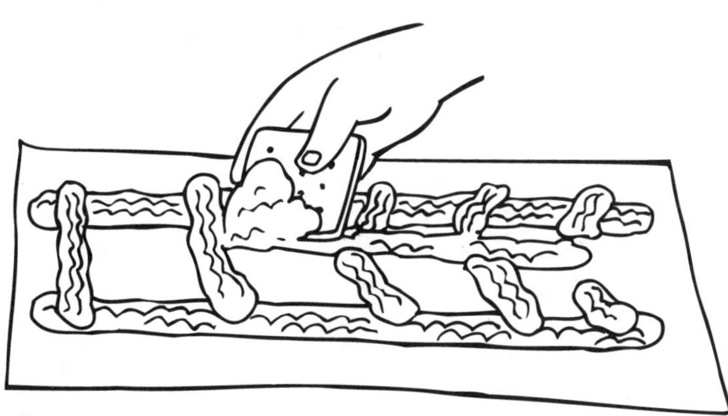

How to Do:
1. Place the wax paper on the cookie sheet.
2. Squirt the cheese in two parallel, straight lines. Add cheese railroad ties between the two lines about 1″ apart.
3. Run the crackers down the track and scoop up the cheese for a snack.

Questions

Q What is the best gift you have ever received?

Q What is the best gift you have ever given to someone?

Q What are some of God's gifts to you?

Q How can you help people who do not have as much as you?

Activity

✔ Set up a "Giving Train" or "Sharing Our Blessings Train" in your classroom. Link several decorated cardboard boxes together. Share the Scripture verses and talk about what they mean. Everything we have is a gift from God and God wants us to share with those around us. Find a local charity that could use stuffed animals, toys, or clothing. Invite your children to bring items to share and place them in the giving train. If at all possible, let the children give the items directly to the charity's representative.

Faith Foundations

Trains are most often used to transport materials, raw or manufactured, from one place to another. They help us move our things. To build a faith foundation in the children during this unit, take a look at what God says about the way to look at the things we have.

Scripture Foundations

Every good and perfect gift is from above, coming down from the Father of the heavenly lights, Who does not change like shifting shadows (James 1:17).

Each man should give what he has decided in his heart to give, not reluctantly or under compulsion, for God loves a cheerful giver. And God is able to make all grace abound to you, so that in all things at all times, having all that you need, you will abound in every good work. As it is written: "He has scattered abroad His gifts to the poor people; His righteousness endures forever" (2 Corinthians 9:7–9).

On the Move ... in Boats

Room Decor

✔ Put a gangplank down as you walk in the door.

✔ Put a large sailboat decoration on the door or large wall space.

✔ Place a lifesaving ring on the door, tied with knotted cord.

✔ Put a large anchor decoration on the door or large wall space.

✔ Place a large boat (real, blowup, or made of heavy cardboard) in the reading corner.

✔ Hang fish netting from the ceiling.

✔ Use the pattern provided (page 38) to make your own border for a bulletin board.

Story Time and Reading Center

Allen, Pamela. *Who Sank the Boat?*

Barton, Byron. *Boats*

Bible story books about boats and/or water

*Brown, Marc. *Marc Brown's Boat Book*

Burningham, John. *Mr. Gumpy's Outing*

Cousins, Lucy. *Noah's Ark*

Crews, Donald. *Harbor*

*Graham, Thomas. *Mr. Bear's Boat*

Hoffman, Patricia A. *The Miraculous Catch of Fish* (CPH, 1999)

Kentley, Eric. *Boat*

Lincoln, Margarette. *Amazing Boats* (*Eyewitness Juniors*, vol. 21)

Pfister, Mark. *Penguin Pete, Ahoy!*

Rand, Gloria. *Salty Dog*

Robb, Andy. *Betty Boat* (CPH 1999)

Rockwell, Anne. *Boats*

Rockwell, Anne. *Ferryboat Ride*

Rotner, Shelley. *Boats Afloat*

Royston, Angela. *Boats and Ships*

Ruane, Joanna. *Boats, Boats, Boats*

*This book is out of print, but may still be available through the Internet, in libraries, or in personal collections.

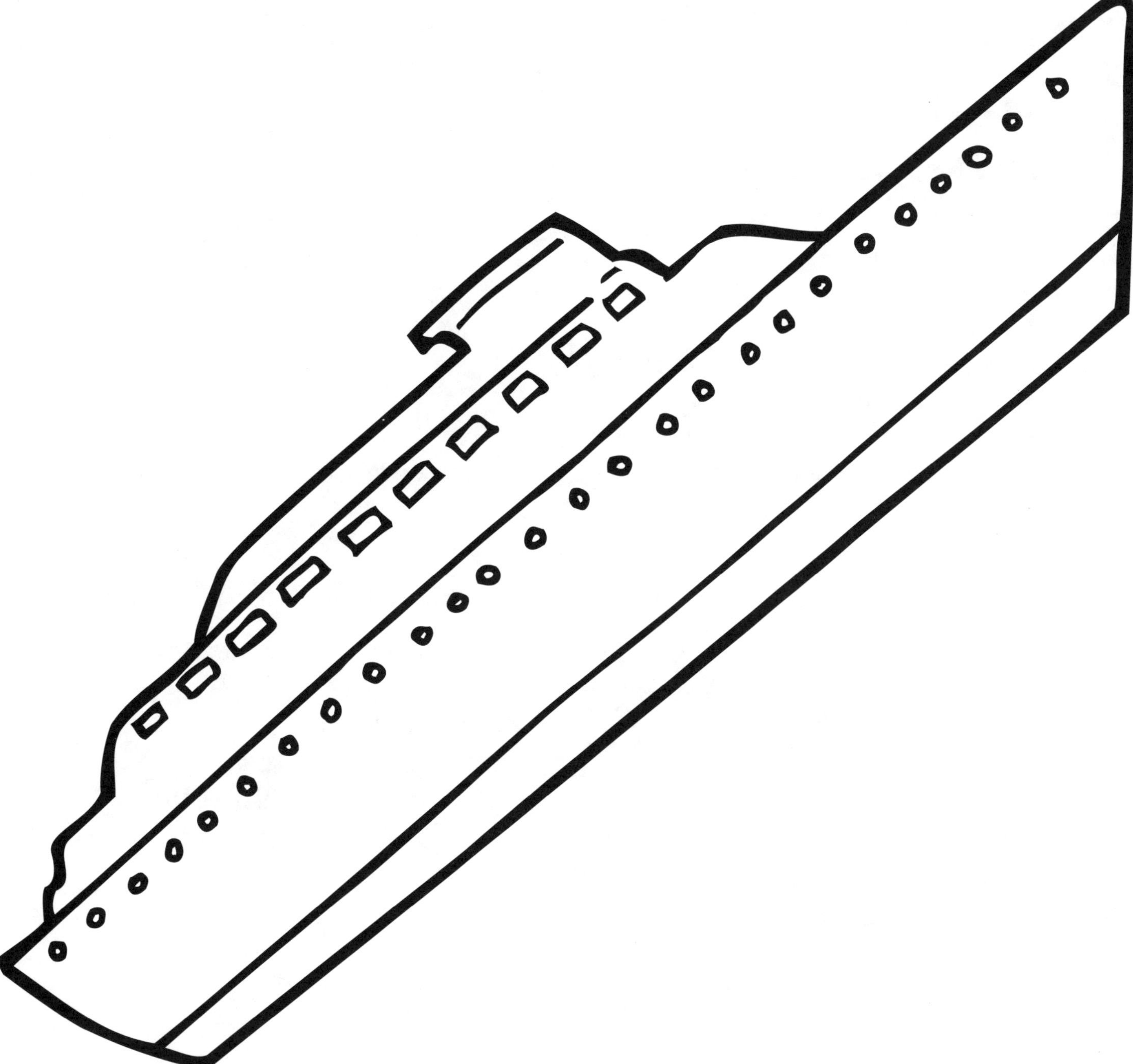

Language and Alphabet Skills

✔ Use the pattern provided to make several fishing boats. Write an uppercase letter on each boat. Write lowercase letters on several fish cutouts. Match the correct fish to its boat by matching upper and lowercase letters.

✔ Make small tagboard canoes. Write an upper or lowercase letter on Popsicle stick paddles. Have the children find the two matching paddles for each canoe.

✔ Use the pattern provided to make large cargo ships. Laminate. Write a letter of the alphabet on each ship. Have the children load the boats with appropriate cargo cut from magazines and catalogs, matching pictures with the ship's letter.

Places to Go
and People to See

✘ Visit a harbor.

✘ Visit a marina.

✘ Tour a boat or ship.

✘ Visit a maritime museum.

✘ Visit a place that sells boats and boating equipment.

✘ Visit a park that has paddle boats.

✘ Invite a boat captain or crew member to speak to your class.

✘ Invite a member of the United States Navy or Coast Guard to speak to your class.

Music! Music! Music!

"Row, Row, Row Your Boat"
"Anchors Aweigh"
"Sailing"
"Blow the Man Down"
"On the Good Ship Lollipop"
"Michael, Row the Boat Ashore"
"Arky, Arky"

Movement

✔ Load the ark two by two. Divide the children into pairs. Give each pair of children the name of an animal to imitate as they climb the plank to the big boat. Once everyone is on the ark, begin to rock back-and-forth and back-and-forth. As the rains begin to pour, wiggle your fingers to resemble rain drops. Everyone looks for a little dove to bring a branch to Noah. Once the rains have stopped and the waters have receded, unload the ark two by two.

✔ Everyone climbs aboard a canoe to ride the rapids. Each child grabs a pretend paddle and begins to paddle down the river. "Whoa! Watch out! Here come the rapids!" Bump up-and-down and side-to-side as you race through the swiftly moving waters towards the waterfall. "Watch out! Jump up and hold your paddle as you ride over the waterfall. Whew! Calm waters." Begin to paddle to shore. Paddle to the dock and get out of the canoe.

✔ Many of the disciples were fishermen. Give every child a (pretend) net to take aboard a big fishing boat. Push the boat out into the water and paddle out to the deep part of the sea. Sway back-and-forth and back-and-forth as the waves hit the boat. Stop the boat in the deep water, cast your nets for fish, and wait. Then pull the heavy net into the boat for your first catch of the day.

Imaginative Play

✘ Sailor caps

✘ Captain hats

✘ Nets

✘ Paddles (cardboard)

✘ Blue vinyl tablecloth or shower curtain to represent water

✘ Cardboard boat made from sections of a large appliance box with a sail made from an old sheet attached to a broomstick

✘ Fishing poles

✘ Galoshes

✘ Cardboard anchor on a rope

✘ Small buckets filled with gummy worms

Making a Floater Sink

You Will Need:

Tub or container for water

Water

Liquid dish soap

Pepper

How to Do:

1. Fill a pie pan or large plastic container about half full with water.
2. Sprinkle pepper on the water. Does it sink or float? (It floats because the water molecules are so close together the pepper can't get through.)
3. Carefully place a drop of liquid dish soap down the side of the pan and watch what happens. (The pepper sinks because the soap creates more space between the molecules.)
4. Rinse the pan thoroughly or use a second pan or container. Repeat the experiment placing the drop of soap in the center. (The pepper sinks in a different pattern than when the soap was placed on the side.)

Home Living Center

✗ Sailor caps
✗ Fishing gear
✗ Waders or tall rubber boots
✗ Plastic fish to prepare in the kitchen
✗ Small packages of goldfish crackers
✗ A real goldfish bowl complete with fish, sunken treasure, and shells

Blocks Center

✗ Include small boats in the center.
✗ Build harbors.
✗ Build docks.
✗ Build lakes by setting up a block perimeter of "rocks."

Sink or Float?

How to Do:

1. Collect a variety of items, making sure to include some that will float and others that will sink. Try to include two of each item. Suggestions: string, straws, a wooden peg, bead, paper clip, ruler (wood and plastic), pencil, crayons, stones, coins, plastic toys, craft sticks, pieces of Styrofoam meat trays, marbles, super balls, and erasers. **Be sure to closely supervise any small items used with young children.**

2. Prepare two charts by dividing two large pieces of paper in half. Label each chart with the headings "sink" and "float." Laminate. Ask the children to place the items under the correct labels on one of the charts, indicating their predictions.

3. Experiment with each item, placing it on the second chart to indicate the results. Compare predictions with actual results. Discuss whether size, weight, or material was a good indicator of whether an object would sink or float.

4. Compare how well objects float or sink in fresh water with how they react to salt water. Take two containers of similar size. Completely saturate the water in one container by stirring in salt until no more will dissolve. Try the "Sink or Float" activity once again. Did some sinkers now become floaters?

Sensory Table

- ✗ Put lots of boats in the water.
- ✗ Put shells in the water.
- ✗ Put plastic fish in the water with magnets.
- ✗ Use play fishing rods with magnets to "go fishing."

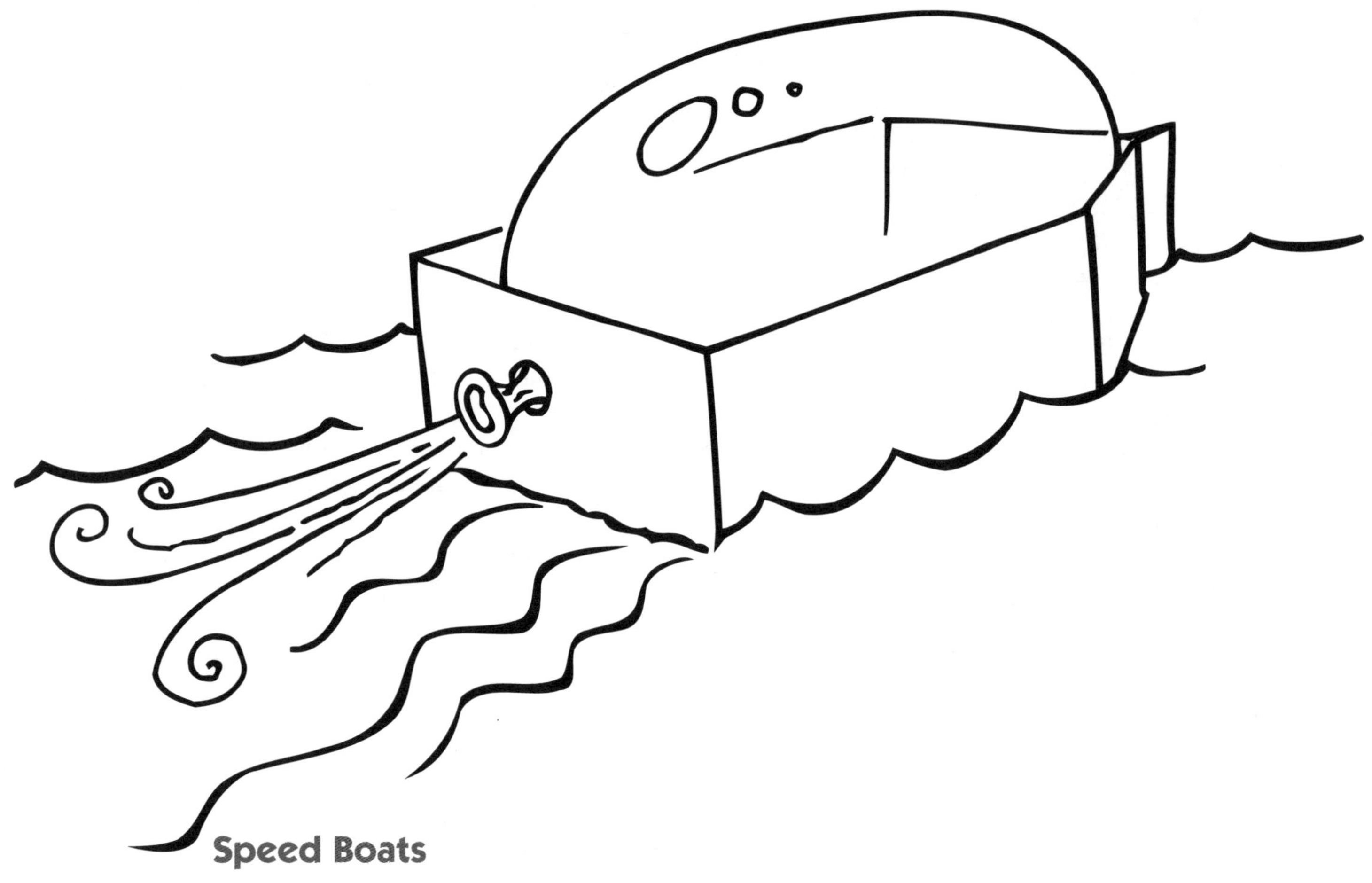

Speed Boats

You Will Need:

1 half-gallon milk carton for every two boats

1 balloon for each boat

Tape or staples, optional

Scissors

Large tub, water table, or child-size wading pool

How to Do:

1. Cut the milk carton in half lengthwise.
   (Reinforce any seams that may be loose
   using the tape or staples if you wish.)
2. Cut a small hole (about ¼") in the back of the carton.
3. Place a balloon in the carton and feed the mouth of the balloon through the small hole.
4. Blow up the balloon but hold it closed. **Do not tie it off.**
5. Place the boat with the inflated balloon in the water. Release the balloon.
6. Race the boats. Experiment with greater and lesser amounts of air in the balloons.
   Compare to a boat that doesn't have a balloon to propel it forward.

Math

- ✔ Use the pattern provided (page 35) to make several ships. Laminate. Write a numeral on each ship. Provide several round stickers (like those used for garage sale pricing) with a second circle drawn in to resemble a port hole. Let the children put the correct number of portholes on each ship.

- ✔ Use the pattern provided (page 37) to make several fishing boats. Laminate. Fasten netting on each side to form a little pocket. Laminate several tagboard or construction paper fish of various colors. Write a numeral on each boat. Have the children put the correct number of fish into the fishing net.

- ✔ Create small ship outlines in three or four colors. Have the children match or form patterns with the colors. Vary the activity by using different kinds of boats (sailboat, canoe, ship) to create the patterns.

- ✔ Use the patterns provided here to make several small tugboats and a matching number of large ships. Write a numeral on each tugboat to correspond to a number of round "porthole" stickers on each ship (or anchors, or smokestacks, etc.). Match each tugboat to the correct ship.

Arts and Crafts

Cork Boats

You Will Need:
Corks of different sizes
Toothpicks
White paper
Colored markers
Scissors
Glue

How to Do:
1. Cut little squares or triangles from the white paper for sails. Decorate them with markers.
2. Glue the pieces of paper together placing the toothpick in the center. Dry thoroughly.
3. Stick the toothpick into the center of the cork to form the sail for the boat.

Super Simple Submarines

You Will Need:

Cardboard
Paper towel tube
Empty spool
Aluminum foil
Brass fastener
Glue
Masking tape
Scissors

How to Do:
1. Cut slits at both ends of the paper towel tube.
2. Pull the slits at either end of the paper towel tube together, forming a rounded end. Tape to hold.
3. Tape the spool to the top of the paper towel tube to form the submarine.
4. Crinkle the foil, unfold, and then wrap the entire submarine.
5. Place the flat side of the brass fastener into the foil. Fold out the two sides of the brass fastener to form the propeller.

Soap Sailboats

You Will Need:

1 bar of Ivory soap per boat
Popsicle sticks
Construction paper
Toothpicks or bamboo skewers
Pencils (optional)
Scissors
Knife **(for adult use only!)**

How to Do:

1. Have the children use a pencil or toothpick to draw the point of the sailboat's bow onto the bar of soap.
2. Using the knife, **an adult** should cut the corners of the soap along the lines the child has drawn.
3. Use the Popsicle sticks to smooth the cut edges into a nice, smooth boat shape.
4. Have the children cut out triangles (provide stencils or patterns) using the construction paper. These will be the sails.
5. Place a toothpick or skewer through each sail and place it on a boat.
6. Hold a class regatta using the boats.

Paper Plate Sailboats

You Will Need:

1 wax-coated paper plate per boat
1 Popsicle stick per boat
Play dough
1 5″ square of paper per boat
Tape

How to Do:

1. Place a blob of play dough in the middle of the paper plate.
2. Stick one end of the Popsicle stick into the play dough.
3. Tape the paper square to the Popsicle stick.
4. Float the sailboats in a large basin of water.

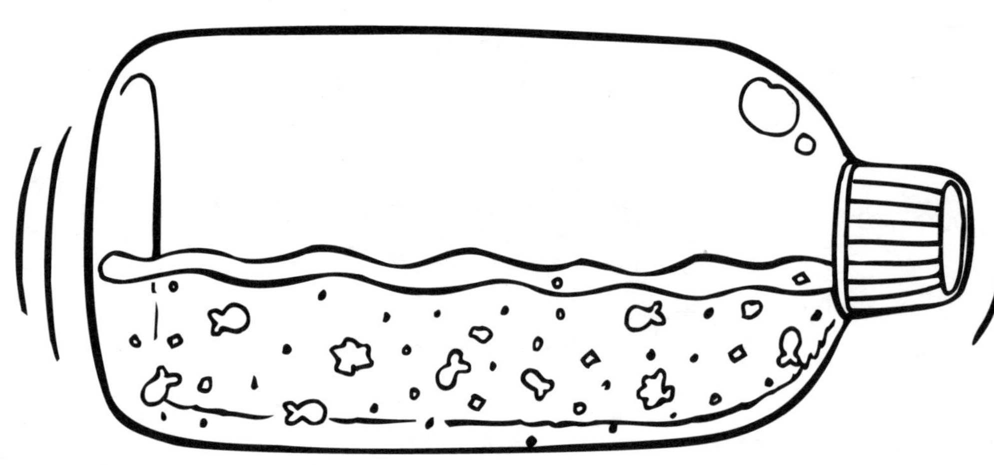

Ocean in a Bottle

You Will Need:
1 16 oz. empty clear plastic
   bottle with screw-on cap
   (soda or baby shampoo
   bottles work well)
Water
   Blue food coloring (green,
      optional)
   Baby oil
Sequins and/or small fish
shapes, optional
Epoxy or SuperGlue

How to Do:
1. Fill the bottle about ⅓ full of water. Add food coloring as desired
   to look like sea water (blue or blue and green).
2. Add a layer of baby oil.
   * You may also enjoy adding small, colorful sequins or plastic
     die-cut fish shapes to the bottle before sealing.
3. Carefully place epoxy or SuperGlue in the bottle cap and screw
   back on. **(Adults only!)**
4. Tip the bottle side to side to watch the wave roll.
   * You may want to set the completed bottles out on a table for children
     to use during their activity/free time.

Snack Time

Bread Boats

You Will Need:
Cutting board
Knife
Ingredients:
Submarine sandwich buns
Favorite sandwich fillings

How to Do:
1. Cut an oval shape out of the top length of a submarine bun.
2. Cut the sail into a triangle to form. Place it in the center of the
   "boat." Fill with your favorite sandwich filling.

Baked Potato Boat

You Will Need:

Baking sheet
Fork
Knife
Oven mitt

Ingredients:

Baked potatoes
Butter
Sour cream
Salt and pepper
Carrot sticks
Small mushrooms

How to Do:

1. Place potatoes on a baking sheet and prick the skins with a fork.
   Bake the potatoes in the oven for 1 ½ hours or until a knife inserts
   easily through the center.
2. Wear an oven mitt and remove the potatoes from the oven. Let cool for 15 minutes.
   Cut the potatoes in half lengthwise, from end to end.
3. Scoop out the potato pulp and place into a bowl.
4. Add the butter, sour cream, cheese, and seasonings to the potato and mix thoroughly.
   Divide the filling in half and refill the potato shells.
5. Stick three carrot sticks in the potato to form the "smokestacks."
6. Push the small mushrooms into the sides of the potato to form the portholes.

Lemon Boats

You Will Need:

Knife
Cutting board
Toothpicks
Spoons

Ingredients:

Lemons
Life Savers, optional
Goldfish crackers, optional

How to Do:

1. Using the cutting board, cut the lemon in half and scoop out all of the inside pulp.
2. Lay one lemon half on its side and cut off a portion of the bottom so that it will sit flat.
3. Cut the other half of the lemon in two. Stick two ends onto a toothpick to form the sail. Stick the
   toothpick sail into the bottom of the other lemon half.
4. Fill the little lemon boat with Life Savers candies or goldfish crackers.

Two by Two

Ingredients:
Animal crackers
Strawberry cream cheese
Strawberries, washed and sliced

How to Do:
1. Sort the animal crackers into pairs.
2. Spread one side of one animal cracker
   with the strawberry cream cheese.
3. Top the strawberry cream cheese with a thin slice of
   strawberry and then with the second animal cracker.

Faith Foundations

Jesus and the disciples were well acquainted with boats. Jesus called Peter, Andrew, James, and John from their work on fishing boats to come and work with Him (Matthew 4:18–22 and Luke 5:4–11). He spoke to crowds from a boat (Luke 5:1–3), traveled on boats across the Sea of Galilee, slept on a boat during a storm He later calmed (Matthew 8:23–25), and walked across the water to join His disciples on a boat (Matthew 14:22–33). He appeared to the disciples after His resurrection as they returned to shore after a discouraging night on a fishing boat.

Scripture Foundations

As Jesus was walking beside the Sea of Galilee, He saw two brothers, Simon called Peter and his brother Andrew. They were casting a net into the lake, for they were fishermen. "Come, follow Me," Jesus said, "and I will make you fishers of men." At once they left their nets and followed Him. Going on from there, He saw two other brothers, James son of Zebedee and his brother John. They were in a boat with their father Zebedee, preparing their nets. Jesus called them, and immediately they left the boat and their father and followed Him (Matthew 4:18–22).

Q What does it mean to follow Jesus?

Q How can you best tell others about Jesus?

Q What would you tell others about Jesus?

Activities

✗ If you have put a large boat in your classroom, sit in it throughout the week to share stories of Jesus and the disciples.

✗ Play "Fishers of People." Set large boundaries such as a fenced outdoor play area or a large open room. Select one person to be the first "fisher." Whenever that fisher tags a "fish," that fish is caught and holds hands with the fisher and any other fish that have been caught. The two outside children become fishers by tagging the other fish. The game is over when the last fish has been caught. The last one tagged can be the first fisher and the game can start again.

✗ Encourage the children to invite friends who may not attend church to go to church with them one Sunday.

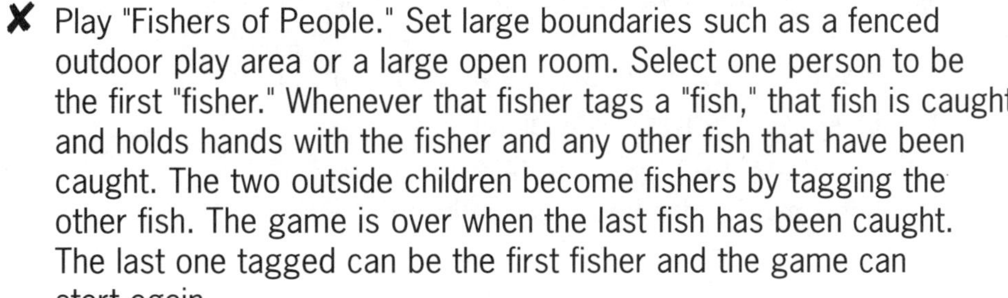
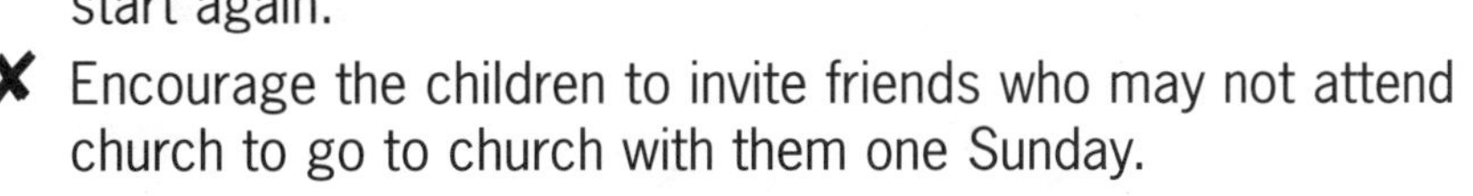

✗ Make a bulletin board display with blue background. Pin a fishing net over the background. Put construction paper fish into the net. Place pictures of the children in the class on the faces of fish. "Caught in the Net of God's Love" could be the title.

On the Move ... on the Highway

Cars, Trucks, Buses, and Other Vehicles

Room Decor

✔ Decorate the door to look like the front view of the vehicle of your choice ... big rig, school bus, car, etc.

✔ Strategically place construction paper "tires" on desks, tables, etc.

✔ Put construction paper windshield wipers on the windows.

✔ Suspend cutouts or small Matchbox cars of various vehicles from the ceiling.

✔ Visit car and construction equipment dealers and collect pictures of cars, trucks, and equipment from old sales brochures to display around the room.

✔ Make a large traffic signal light.

✔ Use the pattern provided here to make your own border for a bulletin board.

Story Time and Reading Center

*Alexander, Anne. *ABC of Cars and Trucks*

Barton, Byron. *Machines at Work*

Barton, Byron. *Trucks*

Becker, Jim and Randy Chewning. *You Can Name 100 Trucks!*

Buller, Jon and Susan Schade. *Toad on the Road*

Crews, Donald. *Truck*

Crews, Donald. *School Bus*

DeSaix, Deborah Durland. *In the Back Seat*

Gibbons, Gail. *Emergency!*

Gibbons, Gail. *Fill It Up!*

Gibbons, Gail. *New Road*

*Koren, Edward. *Behind the Wheel*

*Lenski, Lois. *The Little Auto*

Loomis, Christine. *Rush Hour*

Maccarone, Grace. *Cars! Cars! Cars!*

*Magee, Doug. *Trucks You Can Count On*

*Newton, Laura P. *William the Vehicle King*

*Owen, Annie. *Bumper to Bumper*

Pomerantz, Charlotte. *How Many Trucks Can a Tow Truck Tow?*

Radford, Derek. *Harry at the Garage*

Relf, Patricia. *Tonka Big Book of Trucks*

Robb, Andy. *Rory Racer* (CPH)

Robb, Andy. *Tommy Tractor* (CPH)

Rockwell, Anne. *Cars*

Rockwell, Anne. *Fire Engines*

Rockwell, Anne. *Trucks*

Seltzer, Meyer. *Here Comes the Recycling Truck!*

Siebert, Diane. *Truck Song*

*This book is out of print, but may still be available through the Internet, in libraries, or in personal collections.

Language and Alphabet Skills

✔ Use the patterns provided (pages 50, 51, and 52) to make vehicles out of poster board or construction paper. Laminate. Write an uppercase letter on each vehicle. On milk jug lids write lowercase letters. Match the wheels to the correct vehicle.

✔ Use the bicycle pattern (shown here) to make a bicycle—without tires—on a piece of heavy paper. Draw tires and cut out. On each tire write a letter. Match the uppercase and lowercase letters by pairing the correct wheels on the bicycle.

✔ Label a large Tonka dump truck with a letter of the alphabet. Provide magazines and catalogs for children to "load" with the correct cargo by cutting pictures (or words) beginning with the correct letter and placing them into the truck.

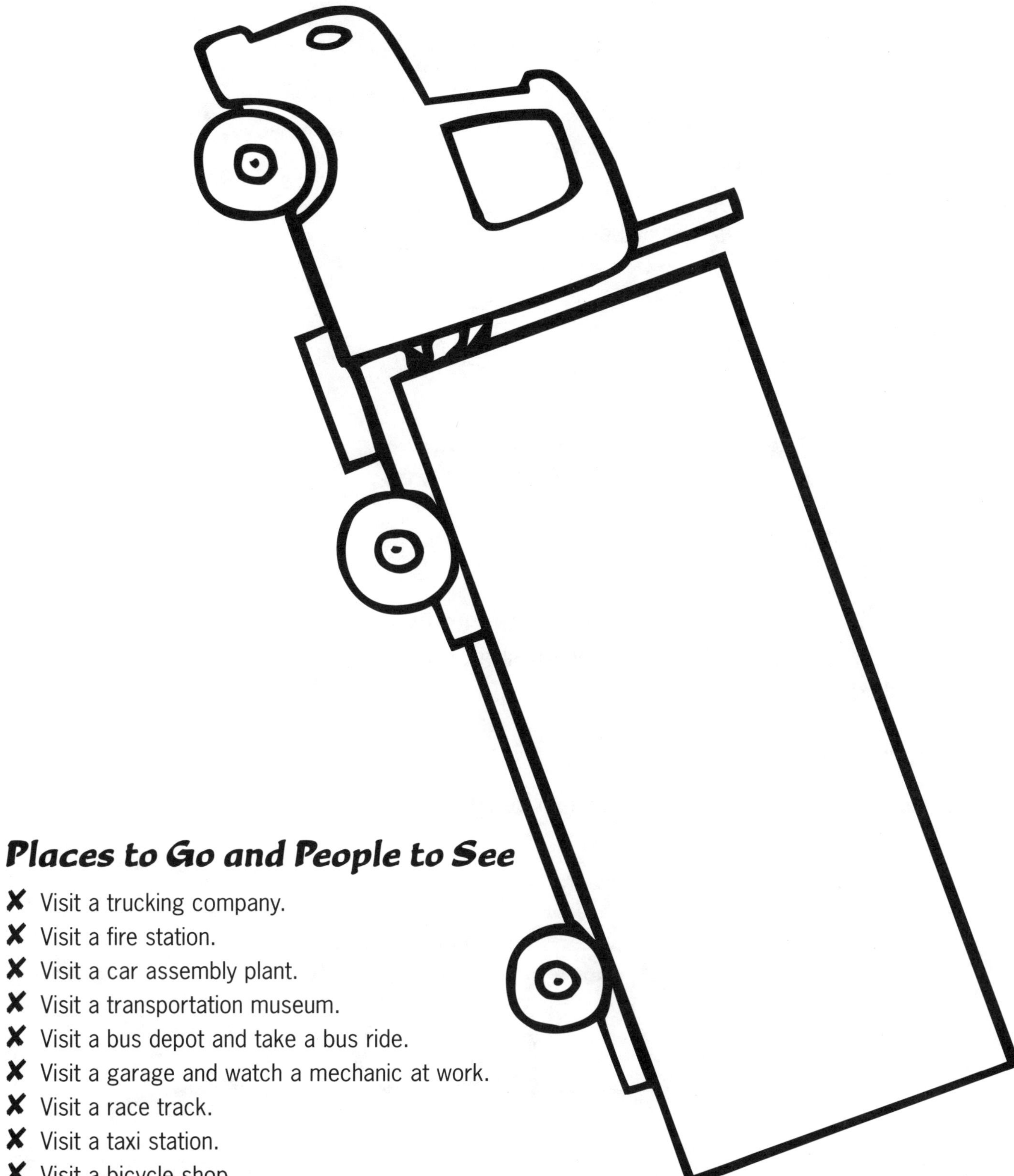

Places to Go and People to See

✗ Visit a trucking company.

✗ Visit a fire station.

✗ Visit a car assembly plant.

✗ Visit a transportation museum.

✗ Visit a bus depot and take a bus ride.

✗ Visit a garage and watch a mechanic at work.

✗ Visit a race track.

✗ Visit a taxi station.

✗ Visit a bicycle shop.

✗ Invite someone who professionally drives a vehicle (bus, fire truck, ambulance, taxi, etc.) to speak to your class.

✗ Invite a mechanic to speak to your class and to show and explain some tools used at work.

✗ Invite someone who works at an auto assembly plant to talk to your class.

✗ Invite someone who works for your city's transportation department to speak to your class.

Music! Music! Music!

"The Wheels on the Bus"
"Bicycle Built For Two"
Music from Sesame Street's
Sing Along Travel Songs CD including:
"Goin' for a Ride"
"Let's Go Driving"
"Drive My Car"
"How Do You Get from Here to There?"
"Stop!"
Improvise familiar tunes with vehicle themes.

"This Is the Way We Drive a Car"

Melody: *"Here We Go Round the Mulberry Bush"*
This is the way we drive a car,
Drive a car, drive a car.
This is the way we drive a car,
When we're on the road.

"She'll Be Driving a School Bus"

Melody: *"She'll Be Comin' Round the Mountain"*
She'll be driving a school bus when she comes.
She'll be driving a school bus when she comes.
She'll be driving a school bus,
Driving a school bus,
She'll be driving a school bus when she comes.

You can substitute any vehicle for "school bus" (i.e., dump truck, fire truck, sports car, etc.)

Movement

- Let each child imitate a tire that is being filled with air. Roll around the room like a tire. Continue to roll around the room until the tire hits a nail on the road. Deflate like a punctured tire. Plug the tire with a gentle pat on the back and inflate like a repaired tire, ready to roll again.

- Race cars go very fast. Have the children form a straight line. Open the door to their race car. Climb inside. Have a seat. Buckle seatbelt. Place hands out in front as if holding a steering wheel. Wave a flag and let the children press the accelerator as hard as they can as the race begins. Bump up-and-down and wave side-to-side, scooting across the floor to the finish line.

- Make cars from boxes for a traffic day. Using cardboard boxes large enough to fit around a child, tape the boxes closed. Cut out a space from the center large enough for a child to stand in. Decorate by adding paint, headlights, taillights, dashboard, steering wheel. Attach rope or straps to the box so that it fits over the child's shoulders and hangs about waist high.

- Modify the activity by making emergency vehicles. Add an upside-down paper cup covered with red paper for an emergency light.

- Modify "Duck, Duck, Goose" to "Truck, Truck, Car." The children sit in a large circle with one child chosen to walk around the circle and gently tap each person on the head. As the child walks, he or she says "truck" each time a sitting child's head is tapped until a child is chosen by saying "car." At that time the tapped child must jump up and chase the "tapper" around the circle until the sitting child's empty space is reached. If the tapper is tagged he or she must begin again. If the tapper reaches the space first then the chosen child then becomes the next tapper.

Out of Gas (outside activity)

✔ Make a gas tank for a tricycle by poking a hole in the bottom of a 2-liter soda bottle.
Tie the bottle, mouth up, to the tricycle using rope or heavy string.
Fill it with water and let the children see how the water runs out "
of the hole in the bottom. They may pedal as long as they
have "gas" in the tank but must stop when the tank is
empty. Designate one area as the gas station. If
they run out of gas before they make it to the
station, they must push the tricycle back.

✔ Play "Red Light, Green Light." Have the children line up along some type of boundary line.
A "traffic director" stands across the room on another line facing them. The children will try to
cross the room to the line on the other side. Children may walk when the director says "green light"
but must stop when the director says "red light." If caught failing to stop or moving while the light is
red, the child returns to the starting line to begin again. The game is over when everyone crosses
the line. (This game may be modified by holding up a red or green construction-paper
signal instead of calling out the words.)

Imaginative Play

✘ Make laundry basket cars by taping four paper plates to the
outside corners of the basket for tires and attaching a paper
plate to one end for a steering wheel. Cut out two each of red
and white construction paper circles. Attach the two white circles to one end for headlights, the two red circles to the other
end for taillights.

✘ Make a dashboard (See "Arts and Crafts" in the Airplane unit
for detailed directions. Modify to resemble a car's dashboard.)

✘ Keys

✘ Driver's licenses

✘ Tool kit

✘ Road maps and atlases

✘ Hard hats (for construction truck drivers)

Home Living Center

- ✗ Keys
- ✗ Road maps and atlases
- ✗ Grocery bags (to carry in from the car)
- ✗ Hard hats (for construction workers to wear to work)
- ✗ Small tire pumps

Sensory Table

- ✗ Fill the table with shaving cream to create snow for Matchbox snowplows.
- ✗ Use sand, sawdust, or dirt with dump trucks and loaders.

Blocks Center

- ✗ Place hard hats in the blocks area.
- ✗ Put Matchbox vehicles in the work area. Use the blocks to build roads and buildings for the vehicles.
- ✗ Put larger dump trucks and other construction equipment in the blocks area. Use the blocks as construction material in the dump trucks, loaders, and cranes.
- ✗ Make or purchase a "city" rug. Put it in the block center along with Matchbox cars and trucks.

Science

- ✗ Freeze large pans or trays of water. Let the children drive the toy cars on the sheets of ice. Compare it to driving on the carpet or the table. Introduce friction.
- ✗ Compare the speed and distance of cars pushed along the floor with those released on an inclined plane.
- ✗ Bring a Hot Wheels racetrack to class that has a loop. Experiment with what happens when the track is flat all the way up to the loop compared to what happens when the car is dropped along a steep ramp. Introduce gravity.

Math

✔ Match shapes to create road signs. You can use circles (railroad crossings), triangles (yield), pentagons (school zone), rectangles (speed limit), or others. Cut sets of each of the shapes. You may either give each child two matching shapes or mix the shapes and let each child find one that matches. Glue the shapes onto opposite sides of a Popsicle stick. Decorate with crayon, marker, or road sign stamps. Set upright using small balls of play dough.

✔ Make the outline of a license plate around the edges of a piece of paper. Copy several kinds of license plates. Set out with number stamps and ink pads or number sponges and washable paint. Let the children make two license plates to go on their box cars.

✔ Use the pattern provided here to make several buses. Cut a generous number of windows on each bus. Laminate. Write a numeral on each bus. Use smiley-face erasers or markers to put the correct number of passengers in the bus.

✔ Use Matchbox vehicles to create patterns.
(For example: car, car, truck, car, car, truck.)
Tape numerals to the tops of Tonka (or other
larger toy) dump trucks. Fill the dumper with
the correct number of items like rocks.

✔ Draw large, thick lines of various lengths on pieces of white paper. Set out a standard "measuring"
vehicle such as several of the same style Matchbox vehicle or several poster board profiles. Let
the children first estimate how many of their chosen vehicle it will take to cover the line. Have them
measure to see if they were correct.

Arts and Crafts

Dashboard

You Will Need:
Sturdy cardboard box at least 18″ wide
Aluminum pie plate or large paper plate
Assorted colors of construction paper
   or various plastic container lids
Brass fasteners
Scissors
Glue
Crayons or markers

How to Do:
1. Turn the box upside down so you will have a flat surface to work on.
2. Poke a hole in the center of the aluminum pie plate and secure it to the box with a brass fastener
   to make a steering wheel.
3. Cut out construction paper circles and write numerals around the perimeter. Draw dials in the
   center for the speedometer, RPM, fuel gauge, and others. Glue the gauges above and to either
   side of the wheel.
4. Cut out three sides of small rectangles in the box to create switches.
5. Once the dashboard is dry, turn it on its side.

Tire Tracks Painting

Let the children roll Matchbox vehicles through thick paint and then roll on the paper to create tire track prints.

Snack Time

Muffin Dump Trucks

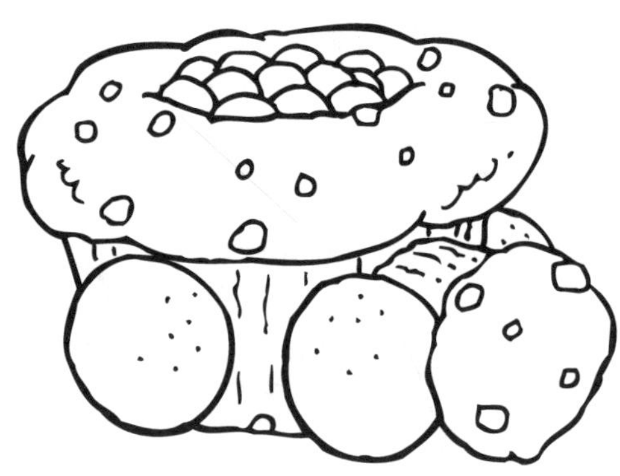

You Will Need:

Wax paper

Plastic knife

Paper plates

Ingredients:

Favorite flavor of ready-made muffins

Icing

Vanilla wafers or round crackers

Favorite items to fill the dump truck (M&M's, Skittles, carrot circles, chopped fresh fruit)

How to Do:

1. Carefully remove the center of each muffin.
2. Use frosting to affix the cut-out center of the muffin to the bottom of the muffin.
3. Use frosting to affix vanilla wafers or round crackers as wheels.
4. Fill the dump truck with favorite things.

Carrot Cars

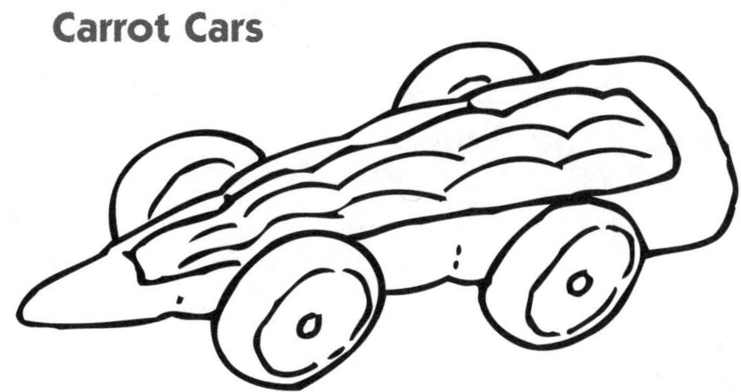

You Will Need:
Cutting board
Knife
Toothpicks

Ingredients:
Carrots
Cheese spread, optional

How to Do:
1. Wash, peel, and slice one carrot.
2. Cut a wedge out of the center length of another carrot.
3. Using a toothpick, affix two of the round carrot slices on each side of this carrot to resemble wheels.
4. Fill the wedge with cheese spread.

Cheesemobiles

You Will Need:
Cutting board
Knife

Ingredients:
2″ thick slice of cheese
Cheese-filled crackers
Squirtable cheese

How to Do:
1. Place the cheese slice on the cutting board.
   Cut ½″ off the back and ½″ off the front.
   Affix to the center of the remaining slice with squirtable cheese to resemble the cab of the car.
2. Place the four cracker "tires" on the cheese car using the squirtable cheese as "glue."

Cookie-on-a-Stick Road Signs

You Will Need:
Cutting board
Knife
Cookie sheet
Lollipop sticks or thick 6″ skewers
Wax paper
* Styrofoam squares, optional
* Craft store fake grass, optional
Ingredients:
Prepared sugar cookie dough
Assorted icings in a tube

How to Do:
1. Cut the cookie dough into ½″ thick slices. Insert the lollipop sticks or skewers into the side of the cookie dough, pushing all the way to the far edge so that the baked cookie will stay securely on the stick.
2. Bake according to package directions. Cool.
3. Cover the counter top with wax paper and place the cooled cookies on a sheet of wax paper.
4. Decorate the cookies with tube icings so that they resemble street signs.

* Cover the Styrofoam with the fake grass. Push the lollipop sticks into the Styrofoam so the signs stand up.

You Will Need:
Paper plates
Small knife or spoon

Ingredients:
Chocolate bars
Large marshmallows
Peanut butter
Graham crackers

How to Do:

1. Place the chocolate bar on a paper plate.
2. Using peanut butter, attach the large marshmallows under the chocolate bar to form wheels.
3. Take two graham cracker squares and break them in half. Glue the edges of the crackers with peanut butter to form a rectangular box.
4. Place the graham cracker box flat-side down at the front of the chocolate bar to form the cab of the truck.
5. Use peanut butter to affix the small marshmallows onto the front of the graham cracker box for the headlights. Smaller marshmallows can also be used for the cargo.

Faith Foundations

Cars and trucks are the most common means of transportation used today to move ourselves from place to place. To build the children's faith foundations during this unit, encourage them to remember that God is with them wherever they go.

Scripture Foundations

O LORD, You have searched me and You know me. You know when I sit and when I rise; You perceive my thoughts from afar. You discern my going out and my lying down; You are familiar with all my ways. Before a word is on my tongue You know it completely, O LORD. You hem me in—behind and before; You have laid Your hand upon me. Such knowledge is too wonderful for me, too lofty for me to attain. Where can I go from Your Spirit? Where can I flee from Your presence? If I go up to the heavens, You are there; if I make my bed in the depths, You are there. If I rise on the wings of the dawn, if I settle on the far side of the sea, even there your hand will guide me, Your right hand will hold me fast (Psalm 139:1–10).

Questions

Q Is there anywhere you can go where God cannot see you or know what you are thinking?

Q Can you name places you go where God is with you?

Q God has promised to always guide us and help us. How can you remember that promise when you are afraid?

Activities

✔ Shadows. Go outside on a sunny day.
Ask the children to look for their shadows.
Can they move somewhere without their shadows?
Where can they go where their shadows will not go
or wait for them? Compare their shadows on a sunny day
to God's presence with them always.

✔ Show the children a globe and talk about all the places
they can travel. Point out that there isn't anywhere on
that globe or off of it that God will not be with them.
Sing "He's Got the Whole World in His Hands."

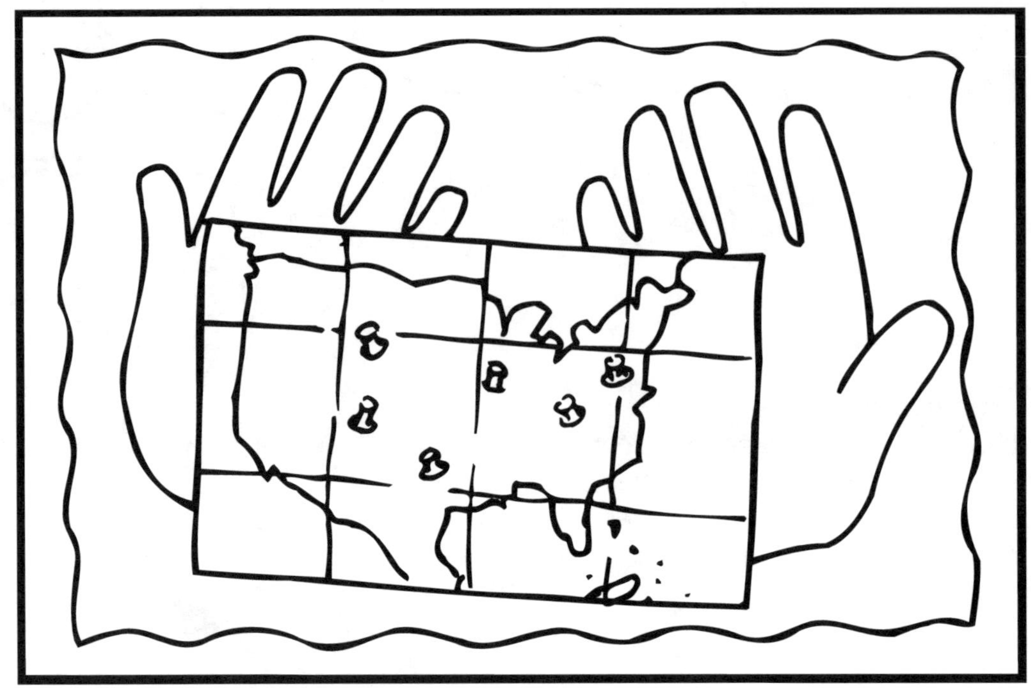

✔ Put a large fold-out world (or USA) map on a bulletin board. Behind the map place two large hands "holding" it. Provide large pins for children and their parents to mark all the places they have been. Title it "The Whole World Is in His Hands."

✔ Play hide-and-seek. After playing, talk about the fact that no matter where we hide, even if our friends can't find our special hiding place, God always knows where we are and is with us. We can never hide from God.